Harassed Husbands

(SECOND REVISED EDITION)

by

KUSUM

M.A.; LL.M.

Former Research Professor

Indian Law Institute

Regency Publications

New Delhi

Division of
DAYA PUBLISHING HOUSE
4760-61/23, Ansari Road,
Darya Ganj, New Delhi - 110 002
Phone: 23245578, 23244987; Fax: (011) 23260116
E-mail: info@regency-books.com
Website: www.regencybooks.com

ISBN 81-87498-64-1

Published by Regency Publications, 20/36-G, Old Market West Patel Nager, New Delhi-110 008 and Printed by Radiant Printers, New Delhi-110 008. Phones: 2571 2539, 2578 3571, 2574 0038

Foreword to the First Edition

This small book deals with a sensitive aspect of matrimonial relations, namely, the plight of harassed husbands, the unsympathetic attitude of persons generally towards them, their problems and the deficiencies of law. Kusum, whose contribution to the literature on matrimonial problems is well-known, has explored a virgin field relying on decided cases and case studies.

While going through the chapter on 'Matrimonial Cruelty' and in particular the sub-topic 'Nagging and Insulting' I was reminded of Socrates who was not spared by his wife. One day, in front of his friend, without any provocation, she went on abusing Socrates. He remained silent and unruffled. Unable to tolerate his cool indifference to her outburst, she poured water on his head. Socrates turned to his friend, remarked: 'rain follows thunder' and walked out of the house with him. It is often said that marriages are made in heaven. These days the incidence of breakdown of marriages on earth is fairly high. The stress and strain of modern life and growing awareness on the part of women of their rights frequently result in incompatibility and mal-adjustment between spouses in many homes, with the concomitant misery and unhappiness not only to the partners and their children, but also to their kith and kin. Kusum's study is revealing indeed in as much as she has demonstrated that matrimonial cruelty is not one sided and there are numerous cases of wife's cruelty towards the husband in one form or the other such as nagging, abuse, neglect, humiliation, infidelity, neglect and abuse of children, threat of suicide and involvement of the husband, his parents and brothers and sisters in criminal cases, denial of conjugal bliss, deprivation of fatherhood, unjustified demand for maintenance, resistance to dissolution of marriage even after it has irretrievably broken down, etc. Her plea for equal treatment of the spouses, without any presumption or prejudice against the husband in matrimonial disputes is not unwarranted, notwithstanding the fact that Judges by their training and tradition tend to take an unbiased and objective view of the facts of each case, even though in most cases they may initially feel instinctively sympathetic towards the wife. The case law noticed in the book shows that husbands do get relief in deserving cases.

Another valid point made by Kusum is that by the time relief comes finally through litigation, in most cases it is too late to settle down with another spouse. The need for speedy disposal is most pressing in respect of matrimonial disputes.

After surveying the existing provisions of law relating to cruelty, dowry deaths, maintenance, custody of children, Kusum suggests significant changes in the law such as a provision for civil damages to the harassed spouse, punishment for making false and malicious complaints against the wife or husband and marriage insurance to cover certain matrimonial risks like victimization, harassment, litigation, etc. In the appendices the relevant provisions of law are set out which facilitate ready reference.

The book is eminently readable and useful to all concerned. It will give not only solace but strength to harassed husbands all over the country. How their spouses will take it is anybody's guess. Seeing the plight of the husbands through the eyes of a female scholar has its own significance. The authoress deserves appreciation for rising above gender bias and making her work objective and authentic.

(P.P. RAO)
Senior Advocate
Supreme Court of India

Dated March 8, 1993

Preface to the Second Edition

Since the publication of the first edition of the book in 1993, there have been innumerable cases of husbands being harassed by wives making false complaints against them. Not that alone, husbands have faced a lot of harassment even from the enforcement and other welfare agencies. Many marriages which could have been saved by objective, sensitive and sensible handling have been ruined because of misuse of certain penal provisions. Rather than mending relations or making the husbands "behave", or "bring them around" rash resort to police and judicial authorities have ended the relationships and back-fired. Even authorities have now started looking at women's complaints with some suspicion. While all sympathy and support was with a woman a few years back, it is unfortunate that credibility is no longer attached to her complaints. While safeguarding her interest, life, property and mental peace still needs to be on top of the agenda in matrimony, the need to ensure that husbands and their families are not needlessly and falsely implicated cannot be underscored. Laws should assist the victimised woman but they should not assist and abet harassment by her of the husband. Fortunately, courts are seized of this phenomenon today and have come to the rescue of harassed husbands.

This small book is aimed at setting the ball rolling in this direction—all in the interest of family and society.

January 2003 KUSUM

Contents

1

Prologue

Woman has always lived in subservience and subjugation. She has suffered injustice, inequality and atrocities within the family as well as outside it. Illiteracy and financial dependence have been the main factors responsible for women's weak position. Times have however, changed and are changing still. Education and literacy amongst girls is on the increase and with that, employment as well. This has contributed towards enlightenment, confidence and financial independence—to some extent though—of women. There is an awareness of rights and dignity of women which society and law have recognised. This is evident from the various provisions in the constitution which provide not only for gender equality but also for enactment of special laws for women. The Constitution also enjoins upon every citizen to denounce practices which are derogatory to the dignity of women. Thus there are special provisions for the welfare of women in most of the general laws and there are also special laws for their welfare. Inspite of all these measures however, atrocities continue to perpetrate on women and amongst the worst type is violence and harassment in marriage. While every marriage has its teething problems which are inevitable because of different backgrounds to which parties belong, temperamental differences and other incompatibilities between the spouses, but these get creased out in course of time. Understanding, perseverance and adaptability can make a marriage happy and successful. During the past few decades however, the evil of dowry has raised its ugly head in the form of dowry harassment to such an extent as to either impel or drive a bride to commit suicide or to eliminate her in the most ghastly manner. Harassment and cruelty to the wife, bride burning and dowry deaths became, and still are, so rampant in our society that special legislative measures had to be taken to combat the evil. However despite laws and awareness campaigns to fight the practice and punish the guilty, women continue to be tortured by dowry hungry husbands and in-laws, in large numbers. This is indeed horrendous and shameful. The agony of the family of the tortured bride can well be imagined. The shock and trauma of those who have lost their daughters cannot be described in words. The entire family is shaken and shattered forever.

While there is no denying the fact that women are still the oppressed class and therefore need protective laws and procedures but what is disturbing is that some laws and procedures have a potential of misuse. As pointed out by Jagjit Singh,[1] "barbarity against married women in India despite stringent laws is one aspect—broadly discussed, debated, analyzed and often becoming headlines. There is another aspect too of the issue—equally sad and disturbing, but undiscussed, undebated, unanalyzed, uncared and unheeded by those who matter. And that is—gross and growing misuse of the anti-dowry laws by estranged wives and their relatives to falsely implicate the innocent husbands and their relatives." There is a growing tendency among women to implicate a large number of members of the husband's family to teach them a lesson. Reason is simple—larger the number of members implicated, higher the chances to extract hefty amount to "settle" the matter.

And this view is shared, apart from the general public, by even the law enforcers and other organisations and agencies set up to protect women's interests. Many husbands are being harassed by unscrupulous wives and their ill-advised parents by involving dowry related laws to the verge of, or infact, driving them to suicide—their number is small though.

A few such cases were narrated by Jagjit Singh.[2] These were "dowry deaths" of three members of a family in Ballabgarh, Haryana, in August 2000, a husband, his young sister and old mother. Unable to meet the growing unreasonable demands by the daughter-in-law and bear the continuous harassment, the old lady, her married son and unmarried daughter aged 22 consumed poison and ended their life. "The ill-fated family was living under continuous and serious threat of being implicated in (false) dowry cases by the daughter-in-law if her demands were not met. The very thought of 'arrest' and the resultant harassment and humiliation shuddered them and the trio decided to commit suicide."

Joginder Singh Ahlawat immolated himself on March 22, 1992 in Delhi. Reason, false complaint of 'dowry demand' by the estranged wife which led him to jail twice. In a note left behind, he held half a dozen persons, including his father-in-law and sister-in-law, responsible for driving him to suicide.

Ravinder Kumar, a bank employee hanged himself on June 12, 1990 in his flat in Maya Puri, Delhi. He objected to his wife's frequent visits to her parents. She retorted by a complaint of dowry against him. Deeply agonised and depressed, he ended his life.

It is submitted that the courts and society should not proceed on an *a priori* assumption that it is always the husband who is guilty. Special statutory provisions are aimed at guarding the interests of wives but unfortunately, they are double-edged weapons and if misused they cause a lot of harassment to the non-complainant. Not that alone, the differences become irreconciliable and there are no chances left of rapprochement between the parties. So great is the fear of being implicated and harassed by a woman on a false dowry charge that the husband and his parents prefer to say good-bye and end the marriage rather than patch up and subject themselves to the risk of getting into trouble and lose their respect and mental peace, and these fears are not wholly unfounded. According to a newspaper report in

1999, in 90% of the cases coming to the Crimes Against Women Cell (CAWC), Nanakpura, Delhi, the lists of dowry items filed by the women are exaggerated. The report also reveals that between 20 to 30% of these cases are such where *istridhana* was actually in possession of women still they lodged complaint against the husbands.

In fact the misuse of dowry and other protective laws is the single largest factor today which has disrupted families and which impede any reconciliatory efforts in cases of marital discord. The result is that there is complete breakdown and in the process all, including the wife whose interest was sought to be protected, suffers.

In this short study, a humble attempt has been made to bring home the point that while women have been and still are being subjected to atrocities of which law and society are aware and measures are being taken to stop this and protect women, yet, there is another side of the coin too. There are husbands as well who are being subjected to harassment. The guilty deserve no leniency and must be deterrently punished. What is important is that the laws and procedures should not be misused. The main purpose behind all welfare, protective and remedial measures is the protection of the woman and peace and harmony in marriage. An irresponsible use of the law and enforcement processes could doom the marriage and the parties. The evil sought to be remedied should not become worse than the evil itself.

ENDNOTES

1. Writer and free-lance journalist.
2. *Ibid.*

2

Cruelty

Cruelty has no parameters. Innumerable are the ways and varieties of conduct which may inflict untold misery and anguish to a spouse against whom it is perpetrated. Constant nagging, neglect, humiliation, false allegations etc. are some forms of cruelty which are sure to destroy one's peace of mind and harmony. A few illustrative cases on the point are indicative of how husband's could be, and have been harassed.

False Accusations

False accusations as regards character or other acts of moral turpitude by one spouse against the other is a clear instance of cruelty. The courts have always been sensitive to the wife's feelings and false accusations against her character have been seriously objected to by the courts. To take an important example—in *Mukund Martan Chitnis* V. *Madhuri Chitnis*,[1] a husband resorted to character assassination of the wife and also filed criminal complaints of theft against her as a result of which search warrants were issued and her house searched. On wife's complaint under section 498-A (cruelty) and section 500 (defamation) of the Penal Code, the High Court convicted the husband on charges under section 498-A and sentenced him to pay a fine of Rs. 30,000 and in default to suffer rigorous imprisonment for six months. On the charge of defamation, he was sentenced to simple imprisonment for two months and a fine of Rs. 6,000. The aggrieved husband came in appeal to the Supreme Court. The Court expressed great concern "to ensure that the wife was adequately compensated for the mental agony, strain and stress that she had undergone on account of the allegations made against her." On the court's advice, a settlement was made under which the husband agreed to deposit Rs. 30,000 as ordered by the High Court. The appeal against conviction for defamation was compounded on the husband agreeing to pay rupees one lakh, alongwith an unquatified apology in the court within one week for the mental strain and stress caused to the wife an account of the various defamatory allegations made against her. As observed by the court, "this should prove to be an eye-opener to those who believe that they can get away by casting aspersions on a woman to serve their ends and to silence her."

Similarly in *Rajee* V. *Baburao*[2] the Madras High Court awarded damages of Rs. 10,000 to the wife against her husband who filed a petition for divorce against her on false charges of adultery only to assassinate her character.

The courts are, however, not insensitive to the husband's feelings also and have granted relief where such conduct and false charges by the wife cause mental anguish and torment to him, and such cases have been in plenty. To take some examples:

In *Kamini Gupta* V. *Mukesh Kumar*[3] the wife called her husband a womaniser and drunkard. She alleged that he brought home girls of ill-repute. These allegations could not be proved. It was held that the charges of immorality levelled by the wife against the husband were reckless in the extreme and entirely baseless and that this "would necessarily cause mental injury to the petitioner husband."

The court held[4]

> "There are no categories of cruel conduct. No compartments. The doctrine of danger of life and limb is no longer in the ascendant ... unending accusations and imputations can cause more pain and injury than a physical beating."

On these facts, the husband was granted divorce.

In *Raj Kishore Prasad* V. *Raj Kumari Devi*,[5] a wife filed a false case against the husband under section 494 of the Penal Code, viz, charging him of bigamy. The court held that this amounted to mental cruelty, particularly since the husband was a government servant and such complaint could lead to serious repercussions on his career.

A wife's complaining in writing to the husband's boss and other colleagues about his extra-marital relations with a lady was construed as the worst type of cruelty on him. The husband was a highly qualified busy scientist spending long hours in his laboratory researching. The disgruntled wife, in order to take revenge, brought into picture an innocent lady student and began a writing campaign involving her.[6]

When the wife of an army man wrote letters to his superiors, to the Prime Minister and to the President of India alleging that her husband was having an affair with a woman for a period of three years and that he should be transferred to a field area and the allegations were proved to be false, the wife was held guilty of cruelty to the husband.[7]

Similarly, in *Pawna Devi* V. *Chuni Lal*[8] a false and unproved allegation by the wife as to husband's second marriage was held to amount to cruelty.

In *S. Vijaylaxmi* V. *S. Bheemreddy*,[9] the wife, alongwith her brother and some muscle men abused her husband and threatened to remove him from service. Apprehending physical harm, he lodged police complaint and obtained anticipatory bail. The wife also filed criminal cases against him as a result of which he was arrested and remanded to police custody. He lost his job also. This clearly constituted cruelty.

A wife's complaining to the husband's superiors levelling false allegations of harassment, physical assault, extra-marital relationship etc. as a result of which he had to seek premature retirement and also suffered acute trauma, depression and psychiatric disorder requiring hospitalisation, was held to be cruelty in *Meenakshi Mehta* V. *Atul Mehta.*[10]

False allegations levelling serious criminal charges as a result of which the husband was called to the police station but ultimately the allegations were found baseless is cruelty;[11] so also where a wife lodged false complaints of dowry demand and the case ended in discharge;[12] and false complaint to police leading to husband's arrest.[13]

In a very recent case[14] where a wife filed a false criminal complaint of dowry demand against the husband under section 498-A of the Penal Code thereby causing him great mental agony the husband sought divorce on ground of cruelty. The wife's appeal against divorce in the Supreme Court was dismissed and she was held to be guilty of cruelty.

In *Manjulabai* V. *Ramachandra,*[15] a wife by her nagging, persistent insults and revolting behaviour made life miserable for the husband. She neglected her household duties and several times the husband had to go to work without food. She broke her bangles, struck her head against the wall and in a fit of rage used to throw away things. She also attempted to set fire to her clothes. The court held that cruelty was proved.

In *Harbhajan Singh Monga* V. *Amarjit Kaur,*[16] the wife not merely refused to do household work but, in the presence of guests forced the husband to clean the dining table, utensils and crockery. She even slapped her husband. At times she used to keep him waiting outside the house for an hour or so on his return from office. She would abuse him in the most filthy language and would constantly threaten him that she would commit suicide and implicate him and his relatives. The husband was granted relief on grounds of cruelty.

Where a wife insisted on the husband's snapping all ties with his parents, and ultimately forced him to live away; never cooked meals and made wild allegations against him and his family, cruelty was established.[17]

A wife threatening suicide, making the husband lose job, insulting him in front of others, tarnishing his and his parent's image, were held enough to imperil his sense of personal safety and mental peace.[18]

In *Rama Kanta* V. *Mohinder Laxmidas Bhandula*[19] a husband's case for divorce on ground of cruelty was based on the wife's bad behaviour, disrespectful attitude towards him and his family members and threats to commit suicide. She had also lodged false criminal complaints against him and his relatives (which ended in acquittal). The same was decreed. In *Alka* V. *R.K. Gautam*[20] it was not a single act or behaviour of the wife which the husband found intolerable but a combination of several, like indifferent attitude towards family members, threat to commit suicide, insulting, and volcanic temperament and deprival of conjugal relations.

How a wife can ruin the husband's career by publicly maligning him is evidenced in *Vimla Ladkani* V. *Dr. Chandra Prakash Ladkani.*[21] The wife was having illicit relations with another man with whom she went around to several places and who was also taking active part in prosecuting her case; she made false allegations against the husband's character in the open court and allegedly got a paper with the lines "*papa sudhar jaiye, nai mummy mat laiye*" (papa mend your ways, don't bring new mummy) purported to have been published on behalf of their children, put near his clinic so as to injure his reputation and medical practice. She also accused him of dowry demand and breach of trust and filed a report in the *mahila thana*. The court granted a decree of divorce to the husband on ground of wife's cruelty.

In *P.K.V. Nair* V. *J. Ammini Amma*[22] a widower with three children remarried but the wife never liked his showing affection to these children. She misbehaved with them, filed false civil and criminal cases against them all and also attempted suicide. All this constituted cruelty towards the husband.

V. Bhagat V. *D. Bhagat*[23] is another significant example indicative of a wife's behaviour inflicting acute mental cruelty on the husband. The husband a practising advocate in the Supreme Court had filed a petition for divorce on ground of wife's adultery. The wife, in her written statement and the questions put by her counsel to him in cross examination made allegations that the petitioner was a mental patient. Statements like he is "suffering from mental hallucination", and, "paranoid disorder", has a "morbid mind and needs psychiatric treatment" were made. In the cross examination the counsel appearing for the wife suggested that the petitioner and several members of her family, including his grand father, are lunatics and that a streak of insanity is running in the entire family. When the petitioner objected to such questions the wife's counsel made the following statement in the open court: "all of your family including your grand father and others are lunatics with streaks of insanity running in the entire family; this is the respondent's case and that is why these questions have been asked." These questions and statements were made by the advocate at the instructions of the respondent. The court construed this as a clear case of wife's cruelty to the husband and dissolved the marriage.

In *Vijay Kumar Jain* V. *Kalpana Jain*,[24] a wife threatened to commit suicide, humiliated the husband by slapping him in public and abused him with filthy language thereby inflicting mental cruelty on him.

In *G.V.N. Kameshwara Rao* V. *G. Jabilli*[25] a husband had been unsuccessfully fighting litigation for 15 years to get out of the marriage on ground of wife's cruelty. He was an academically highly qualified person with two doctrates and the wife also was a post graduate and working as a lecturer at the time of marriage. The husband was working in the U.S.A. and the wife joined him there after six months. There were problems and quarrels right from the beginning. The wife was always quarrelling and behaved in a very insulting manner; humiliating the husband in presence of outsiders and creating scenes, not doing any household work, refusing to share bed etc. After sometime she returned to

India with their daughter and the husband did not even know where they were until he made enquires and found out. She also filed criminal complaints to the police alleging that she was badly beaten by him and his mother. They were called to the police station and had to be there for more than 10 hours. The police however refused to register any complaint as they did not find any *prima facie* case. On these facts the court found that the husband who was holding a position in life must have suffered humiliation, and acute mental cruelty in the hands of the wife and so was entitled to a decree of divorce.

Neglecting Husband in Illness

A wife who does not attend on her seriously ailing husband can cause immense mental cruelty to him which has been judicially recognised as well. In *Rajinder Singh* V. *Tarawati,*[26] a husband who was in the army met with a serious accident and was admitted to the Military Hospital in Assam. The wife was informed about it but she did not go to see him. After being hospitalised at Assam, for eight months, he was shifted to the Delhi Military Hospital but there also the wife did not care to visit him. She was so indifferent inspite of the fact that she knew that he was on the "serious sick list". This was considered to be cruelty and the husband was granted divorce.

Physical Violence

Some wives are capable of using physical force also. For instance, in *N. Sreepadachar* V. *Vasantha Bai,*[27] a wife abused the husband in a bus, caught hold of his collar, made him cook food for her and when he served the food, she threw the plate on his head saying that the same was not properly cooked. She also stated before others that she wished that he may be killed in an accident so that she may get his insurance and provident fund claims. Likewise, in a case from Punjab and Haryana, a robust heavy built and quarrelsome wife used physical violence against her husband and his relatives.[28]

A sordid example of acute mental and physical cruelty inflicted by a wife on the husband is evinced in *Savitri Bal Chandani* V. *Mulchand Bal Chandani.*[29] Whenever she wanted to compel the husband to do something, she would instigate the son to grab the testicles of her husband and squeeze them.

In a recent case from Rajasthan, a wife asked the mother-in-law to transfer the house in her name which the mother-in-law declined to do. The wife not only misbehaved with her and turned her out of the house but had her husband beaten up by her brothers. She also made false allegations of dowry demand. This was treated as cruelty by the wife.[30]

Cruelty to Children

A wife can cause deep anguish to the husband by being cruel and indifferent to the children. In one case, the wife deserted her husband leaving a two month old infant behind. The husband, alongwith some relatives went to her village and requested her to come back but she refused. In the alternative, they requested her to keep the baby to which also she did not agree. The child died. This was construed as cruelty to the husband.[31]

Denial of Sex

Sex plays a very important role in marriage and has been considered to be an important factor in the success or failure of a marriage. The following observations of Justice Rajindar Sachhar in *Nijhawan* V. *Nijhawan*[32] are significant in this context.

> "Marriage without sex is an anathema. Sex is the foundation of marriage and without a vigorous and harmonious sexual activity, it would be impossible for any marriage to continue for long.... It must be recognised that nothing is more fatal to marriage than disappointment in sexual intercourse."

Denial of normal sexual relations is thus, another species of cruelty. Thus where a wife did not allow her husband to consummate the marriage, went abroad without informing him, nor met him after return, it was held to be cruelty.[33]

Deprivation of Parenthood

Parenthood is a normal natural desire of every human being.[34] A spouse who deprives the other of this pleasure and desire would be causing great mental agony to that other spouse. Such cruelty may be inflicted by either spouse towards the other. Thus a spouse may resort to sterilisation or *coitus interreptus* or a wife may refuse access to the husband or terminate her pregnancy thereby depriving the other of parenthood. The courts have, at times, made a distinction between such attitude or conduct of the wife and that of the husband. For instance, in *Fowler* V. *Fowler*,[35] the wife refused to have children and insisted on the use of contraceptives as a result of which the husband's health suffered. The court however, held that the wife was not guilty of cruelty unless her conduct was intended to inflict misery on her husband. A distinction was made between a wife's refusal to have children and a husband's similar refusal. The court observed.[36]

> If a man takes contraceptive measures against the will of his wife ... so as to prevent her having children, without reasonable excuse for so doing, then it is easy to infer that he does it with intent to inflict misery on her.... But when a wife herself takes contraceptive measures, or asks her husband to take them, her conduct can often be attributed to fear of the consequences to herself, without any intention of injuring him. She fears the pains and risk of child birth. This is very unnatural and unfortunate, but it is not cruelty unless she has also an intention to inflict misery on her husband.

In *Forbes V. Forbes*[37] and *P* V. *P*[38] however, the court took a different view. In *Forbes*, the wife insisted on the use of contraceptive to avoid having children. All efforts on the part of the husband to persuade the wife failed so he filed a petition for divorce on ground of cruelty. The court observed:[39]

> "Quite apart from the exhortation in the solemnisation of matrimony that, first ... marriage was ordained for the procreation of children, I cannot ignore the fact that it is a natural instinct in most married men to propagate the species and to bear the responsibilities and enjoy the comforts of their own children. If a wife deliberately and consistently refuses to satisfy this natural and legitimate craving, and the deprivation reduces the husband to despair, and affects his mental health, I entertain no doubts that she is guilty of cruelty."

Likewise in *P* V. *P*[40] where the wife was suffering from a psychological fear of conception and child birth which she could not overcome and as a result of which she deprived the husband of normal sex life and the opportunity of becoming a father, the court held that it amounted to cruelty on the husband.

Bravery V. *Bravery*,[41] *Knott* V. *Knott*[42] and *Sheldon* V. *Sheldon*[43] are instances where a husband inflicted cruelty on wife by depriving her of motherhood by undergoing sterilisation operation, by practising *coitus interruptus* and by depriving her of normal sex life, respectively.

In the context of a harassed Indian husband, a reference may be made of a few cases. In *Satya* V. *Siri Ram*[44] a wife got her pregnancy terminated twice against the wishes of her husband and his family who were very keen to have a child. The husband tried his best to persuade his wife but failed. The court held that the conduct of the wife amounted to cruelty. Likewise in *Sushil Kr. Verma* V. *Usha*[45] a wife's terminating her first pregnancy without husband's consent was held to amount to cruelty.

Such cases are not unusual. The wife may have her own reasons for not having a child. The Medical Termination of Pregnancy Act, 1971 also gives her a right to terminate her pregnancy and she does not need her husband's consent for that. Moreover, a woman has a right over her own body, life and health and she may be suffering from fears or apprehensions—genuine or imaginary. Nonetheless it cannot be denied that progeny and parenthood is a very legitimate desire and the courts would definitely give due regard to the husband's sentiments in this respect.

Malafide Obstacles in Judicial Proceedings

A very common form of harassment which is increasing day by day is the recalcitrant wife's obstacles in the way of a divorce even when she has no intentions of living with him. There are innumerable cases where a wife has made criminal complaints against the husband and her relatives leading to their arrest, she has also got back her *stridhan* and other belongings and yet she resists the divorce petition filed by the husband. She neither wants to live with him nor give him "freedom" but only wants to harass him and "teach him a lesson". In cases where the wife has no plans to remarry, this is invariably the position. Infact, so long as breakdown of marriage is not introduced as a ground for divorce in our matrimonial laws, the courts should allow divorce in cases where a husband who, on wife's complaint is facing criminal trial or has been suspended from service, because such marriage is extinct for all practical purposes. A couple cannot be expected to live happily after all this; it could rather lead to more vindictiveness and bitterness and end up in disastrous consequences.

Thus we see that the parameters of cruelty are wide enough to include any unreasonable act or behaviour by one spouse which may cause agony, physical or mental pain to the other and which the courts think would be unfair to expect that other spouse to live with. It cannot however be denied that there is a lot of subjectivity involved in continuing cruelty. Apart from that, at times the technicalities of law come in the way of giving effective relief to the complaining spouse. For instance, in *P* V. *P*[46] a husband filed for divorce on the ground of adultery and cruelty of the wife. He engaged the assistance of a detective agency to watch the movements of his wife and collected considerable evidence. The judge was convinced of the dubious manner and suspicious circumstances in which the wife moved; he also agreed that these would arouse anybody's suspicion and doubt her innocence and remarked, "there is enough evidence to show that she was carrying on with the second respondent," yet relief was not granted on technical grounds *viz* absence of direct proof. The judge remarked:[47]

> "It is possible that it was a preliminary step to adultery and may ultimately have resulted in adultery but it cannot be said that the incident proved that adultery took place."

Against this, the husband went in appeal.[48] After referring to various authorities cited by the counsel for the husband, the court was convinced that the wife was guilty of cruelty nonetheless the appeal was dismissed. The court said:[49]

> However, inspite of that, there is no evidence at all, not a single word in the evidence that the conduct of the 1st respondent [the wife] has caused any danger to the health of the petitioner or has given rise to any apprehension of such danger. Such an allegation is made in the petition but there is no evidence to the effect given in the examination-in-chief.... In my view looking at the circumstances of the case, though it is unjust to compel the petitioner to continue his marriage with the 1st respondent, it is unfortunate that the law being what it is, I have no alternative but to dismiss the appeal.

In *Dastane* V. *Dastane*[50] the parties had been litigating for over a decade. The wife tried to injure the reputation of the husband in every possible way, took delight in causing misery to the husband and his relatives, and constantly nagged him. The husband's petition for separation on the ground of cruelty was dismissed on the technical ground of condonation as there were short spells of reconciliation to try if the marriage could work.

J.L. Nanda V. *Veena Nanda*[51] is another case where there was long drawn litigation with ultimately no effective relief. The parties had problems in the early days of marriage but somehow continued to stay together for about ten years. They practically parted company in 1971. The husband alleged that from the very beginning the wife did not like to live in the joint family. She used to behave in a peculiar manner created ugly scenes, indulged in quarrels and nagging and ultimately forced him to shift to a government allotted house and live separately from other family members. Her behaviour did not change and the relations became further embittered. The husband suffered a nervous breakdown for which he had to be hospitalised for about 45 days. Under these circumstances, the trial court granted the decree but on appeal both the single judge and the Division Bench of the Delhi High Court dismissed the suit. The husband went in appeal to the Supreme Court and the court found no reason to interfere. It remarked.[52]

> Sometimes the temperament of the parties may not be conducive to each other which may result in petty quarrels and troubles although it was contended by the appellant that he had to suffer various ailments on account of this kind of behaviour meted out to him by the wife; but it could not be held on the bases of any material that ailment of the appellant was the direct result of her conduct."

Thus despite a legal battle for about two decades the couple had to remain legally wedded but practically divorced.

ENDNOTES

1. 1992 S.C. 1804.
2. AIR 1996 Mad. 262.
3. AIR 1985 Del. 221.
4. *Id.* at 224.
5. AIR 1986 Pat. 362.
6. *A.S. Paintal* V. *Iris Paintal* AIR 1986 Del. 60.
7. *Aruna* V. *Ramesh Chand* AIR 1988 All. 239.
8. (1998) 2 DMC 1 (DB).
9. AIR 1998 AP 296.
10. AIR 2000 H.P. 73; see also *Abha Agarwal* V. *Sunil Agarwal* AIR 2000 All 377; *Surbhi Agarwal* V. *Sanjay Agrawal* AIR 2000 MP 139; *Bhagwanti* V. *Lachmandas Panjwani* AIR 2000 MP 190.

11. *S. Banerjee* V. *S.N. Banerjee* AIR 1990 Cal. 367.
12. *Smt. Kanta Sachdeva* V. *Devidas* (1998) 2 DMC 368.
13. *Suresh Bala* V. *Maj. G.S. Bala* AIR 1983 Del. 230.
14. *Indirani* V. *A. Muthuswamy*. Supreme Court order dated Jan. 23, 2002.
15. 1972 MPLJ 692.
16. AIR 1986 MP 41.
17. *Pushpa Bai* V. *Kamal Jain* (1986) IDMC 389 (MP).
18. *Nathu Lal* V. *Nathi Bai* (1997) IDMC 598 (Raj.).
19. AIR 1996 P. and H. 98.
20. AIR 1996 Del. 276.
21. AIR 1996 MP 86.
22. AIR 1987 Ker. 170.
23. AIR 1994 S.C. 710 (from Delhi).
24. (2000) IDMC 399; see also *Rama Kanta* V. *Mohinder Laxmidas Bhandula* AIR 1996 P. and H. 98.
25. (2002) 2 SCC 296.
26. AIR 1980 Del. 213.
27. AIR 1970 Mys. 232.
28. *Rani Devi* V. *Hussainlal* AIR 1988 P. and H. 65.
29. AIR 1987 Del. 52.
30. *Pramila Bhatia* V. *Vijay Kumar Bhatia* AIR 2000 Raj. 362.
31. *Gurcharan Singh* V. *Sukhdev Kaur* AIR 1979 P. and H. 98.
32. AIR 1973 Del. 200 at 209.
33. *Abha Gupta* V. *Rakesh Gupta* (1996) I DMC 71 (P. and H.) see also, *G.V.N. Kameshwar Rao* V. *G. Jabilli* (2002) 2 SCC 296; *Rakesh Pathak* V. *Kiran Pathak* (1986) I DMC 443 (MP); *Shakuntala* V. *Om Prakash* AIR 1981 Del. 53.
34. See Kusum "Deprivation of Parenthood: Whether Amounts to Matrimonial Cruelty" 1978 (II) Madras Law Journal Reports 28–30.
35. (1952) 2 TLR 143.
36. *Id.* at 148.
37. (1955) 2 All E.R. 311.
38. (1965) 2 All E.R. 456.
39. *Supra* note 37 at 314.
40. *Supra* note 38.
41. (1954) 3 All E.R. 59.
42. (1955) 2 All E.R. 305.
43. (1966) 2 All E.R. 257.
44. AIR 1983 P. and H. 252.
45. AIR 1987 Del. 86.
46. AIR 1982 Bom. 498.
47. *Id.* at 505.
48. AIR 1983 Bom. 8.
49. *Id.* at 12.
50. AIR 1975 S.C. 1534.
51. AIR 1988 S.C. 407.
52. *Id.* at 408.

3

Protective Penal Provisions: A Double-edged Weapon

The most common and extreme form of exploitation of a husband and his family by a wife and her family is by making false charges of harassment for dowry, ill-treatment and abetment to suicide.

Dowry is a deep-rooted social evil in our society. However during the past few years it has taken a very ugly turn. Dowry deaths—either by way of suicide by a harassed wife or murder by the greedy husband and in-laws—has indeed become a cause of great concern for parents, legislators, courts and the society as a whole. There is no denying the fact that this evil needs to be curbed with the stringentmost laws. In 1961 the Dowry Prohibition Act was passed to prohibit giving or taking of any valuable security or property "in consideration of marriage". At the same time, presents in the form of cash, ornaments, clothes and other articles were exempted from the purview of the definition of dowry. There were several other loopholes also in the law. Consequently amendments were made to the Act in 1984 and 1986 to make it more stringent. The definition of dowry has been widened to include any property or valuable security given or agreed to be given at, or before, or at any time after the marriage. This continued demand for dowry has been brought expressly within the mischief of the law. Penalties have also been raised. Besides, the offences relating to dowry have been made cognizable, non-bailable and non-compoundable. The burden of proof of innocence rests on the accused. However, despite such laws, the evil continues unabated and many innocent wives suffer or commit suicide or are murdered. To control and check victimisation of wives due to dowry, Parliament introduced certain amendments to the criminal laws also. As pointed out by the Supreme Court in *Brij Lal* V. *Prem Chand*:[1]

> "The degradation of society due to the pernicious system of dowry and the unconscionable demands made by greedy and unscrupulous husbands and their parents and relatives resulting in an alarming number of suicidal and dowry deaths by women has shocked the legislative conscience to such an extent that the legislature has deemed it necessary to provide additional provisions of law—procedural as well as substantive—to combat the evil and has consequently introduced sections 113-A and 113-B in the Indian Evidence Act and sections 498-A and 304-B in the Indian Penal Code."

The object of all these sections is to protect married women and in case of suicide or murder, there is a presumption that the husband and his relatives are the offenders.

Cruelty and Harassment

The offence of cruelty, both mental and physical, by husband or relatives in connection with unlawful demands for property is specifically dealt with in section 498-A of the penal code. The minimum punishment prescribed in such cases is three years of imprisonment and fine. The court can take cognizance of offences under this section upon police report or upon complaint by the aggrieved woman or her relatives.[2] In case of an unnatural death of a woman within seven years of her marriage, it is mandatory for the police to send the body for post-mortem. The inquest by a magistrate into the cause of death becomes necessary in such cases under section 176 of the Cr. P.C., either instead of, or in addition to, the investigation held by police officers.

Section 498-A says

"Whoever, being the husband or the relative of the husband of a woman subjects such woman to cruelty shall be punished with imprisonment for a term which may extend to three years and shall also be liable to fine.

Explanation: For the purpose of this section, cruelty, means:

(a) any wilful conduct which is of such a nature as is likely to drive the woman to commit suicide or cause grave injury or danger to life, limb, or health (whether mental or physical) of the woman; or

(b) harassment of the woman where such harassment is with a view to coercing her or any person related to her to meet any unlawful demand for any property or valuable security or is on account of failure by her or any person related to her to meet such demand."

The law of evidence, under which as a matter of general rule, a fact has to be proved by the person who makes an allegation, makes an exception in order to make section 498-A more meaningful and stringent. Thus under section 113-A of the Evidence Act which was introduced in 1983:

"When the question is whether the commission of suicide by a woman had been abetted by her husband or any relative of her husband and it is shown that she had committed suicide in this period of seven years from the date of her marriage and that her husband or such relative of her husband had subjected her to cruelty, the court may presume, having regard to all the other circumstances of the case, that such suicide had been abetted by her husband or by such relative of her husband.

Explanation: For the purposes of this section cruelty shall have the same meaning as in section 498-A of the Indian Penal Code."

Dowry Death

Section 304-B of the Penal Code and section 113-B of the Evidence Act deal with the offence of dowry death and the presumption in such cases.

Section 304-B[3] of the Penal Code says:

(1) "where the death of a woman is caused by any burns or bodily injury or occurs otherwise than under normal circumstances within seven years of her marriage and it is shown that soon before her death she was subjected to cruelty or harassment by her husband or any relative of her husband for, or in connection with any demand for dowry, such death shall be called "dowry death", and such husband or relative shall be deemed to have caused her death.

Explanation: For the purposes of this sub-section, "dowry" shall have the same meaning as in Section 2 of the Dowry Prohibition Act, 1961.

(2) Whoever commits dowry death shall be punished with imprisonment for a term which shall not be less than seven years but which may extend to imprisonment for life."

Under Section 113-B[4] of the Evidence Act,

"When the question is whether a person has committed the dowry death of a woman and it is shown that soon before her death such woman had been subjected by such person to cruelty or harassment for, or in connection with, any demand for dowry, the Court shall presume that such person had caused the dowry death.

Explanation: For the purpose of this section, "dowry death" shall have the same meaning as in section 304-B of the Indian Penal Code."

It may be pointed out here that section 498-A, IPC and section 113-A of the Evidence Act were challenged in 1987 in *Satyanarayana* V. *Soundarya Valli*.[5] A wife mentally harassed and physically tortured by her husband and his mother accused them of cruelty under section 498-A. On receiving the summons, the husband filed a writ petition assailing the constitutional validity of sections 498-A and 113-A. The same was dismissed by the single judge against which an appeal was filed before the Double Bench.

It was contended that the definition of the word cruelty under section 498-A should be explicit, specific and definite, "but it is delightfully vague and wide of the mark. Therefore it is arbitrary."[6]

The next contention was that the husband and his relatives cannot be singled out for the purpose of legislation under the Amendment Act. "There is no reasonable relation, nor any nexus to single them out from the general body of offenders. Accordingly, it is obnoxious to Art. 14 of the Constitution.[7]

It was further argued that the procedure prescribed lugging the husband or relatives of husband for the offence of cruelty is violative of Articles 20 and 21 and thus offending right to life.

And lastly, that section 113-A which puts the burden of proving innocence on the accused, is in negation of the criminal jurisprudence and settled notion of law that the accused is presumed to be innocent and the burden is always on the prosecution to establish beyond reasonable doubt that the crime has been committed by the offender. Hence section 113-A of the Evidence Act is violative of Article 14 of the Constitution.

The court did not accept these contentions. The term cruelty is clearly defined under section 498-A as such "wilful conduct which is of such a nature as is likely to drive the woman to commit suicide or to cause injury or danger to life, limb or health, whether mental or physical." The section further explains harassment of a woman to coerce her or any other to meet any unlawful demand for property as cruelty. Thus the term "cruelty" is not used in an arbitrary manner. According to the court the term must be "considered in the light of the object the statute seeks to achieve and the purpose which it seeks to subserve and the context in which the definition is made."[8]

As regards the other contention that the husband or the relatives of the husband cannot be treated as a class apart from general class of offenders, the court observed that the relatives and/or the husband are often the prime offenders or abettors. The inmates of the house have special knowledge regarding wilful conduct or the harassment or cruelty etc., meted out to the married woman. Therefore, in a given situation, either the husband or the in-laws or the relative or relatives of the husband may be prime offenders or abettors or one or all of them may be jointly or individually responsible for commission of the crime. Thus they constitute a class by themselves apart from the general offenders. The classification has reasonable nexus and bears just relation to the object achieved.[9]

As regards the objection to shifting the burden of proof on the husband and his relatives, the court observed that "the inmates have special knowledge of the circumstances under which the offence of suicide is committed or cruelty or harassment is caused leading to the commission of suicide. Therefore the legislature drew presumptive evidence in favour of the prosecution. It does not relieve the prosecution to prove its case on the touch-stone of proof beyond reasonable doubt."[10] Thus there is a reasonable and just relation to the object sought to be achieved and therefore the presumption drawn under section 113-A of the Evidence Act is not violative of Article 14 of the Constitution.

The court reiterated the point that there was no violation of the Constitution. "The presumptive evidence under section 113-A of the Evidence Act has been drawn keeping in view the paramount social interest as against the interest of a specified class of offenders, viz., husband or his relatives."[11]

Role of Women's Cells (Police)

Apart from special laws to meet the situation of steep rise in the incidence of crimes and atrocities against women, special police cells have also been set up to help women. The first such cell was set up in 1983 at the police headquarters at Delhi. It was known as the Anti-Dowry Cell. The working of the cell for two years revealed that every problem in the family was attributed to dowry demand by the husband and his people. Every case of suicide or death of a wife was considered to be a dowry death. Thus, dowry was used as a scape-goat. A woman who felt harassed due to any other reason not even related to dowry, e.g., husband's habit of drinking or an extra-marital affair etc. would take the plea of dowry and make a complaint to the women's cell. The enforcement authorities were not oblivious of this fact. In 1985 the name of the cell was changed from Dowry Cell to "Crimes Against Women Cell." Thus now not only cases of dowry but all sorts of harassments or atrocities on women are looked into by this cell. In fact, however, most of the problems are still attributed to dowry. Cases are not immediately registered. Summons are sent to the other parties and inquiries made. There are a couple of sittings in which attempts are made to sort out the problems. If it is a case of *stridhana* which the wife wants back and the husband refuses to return, the cell tries to help the wife. Quite often the case is referred to court where it takes its own time.

Besides these special police cells, many women's organisations have also come up to help women in distress. Barring very few which are well established with mature, experienced and objective staff, many of these organisations have had and are having, a negative impact on marital relationship. Though militancy is necessary in such cases but not at the cost of logic and expediency. The problem is aggravated rather than mitigated by holding *dharnas* or shouting slogans etc.

There is no denying the fact that all these statutory and other special measures are laudable. Women do need security and protection against torture and harassment by the husband and his family. What however is disturbing is the misuse of these provisions. Dowry is being made a scape-goat for all problems in the family. A man whose wife is not happy in her marriage for whatever reasons is placed in a very vulnerable position. True, in many of these cases a woman may be a victim of dowry harassment but surely not all cases of unhappy or strained relations can be attributed to dowry demands. A woman may feel harassed and frustrated for many other reasons also like, lack of privacy or independence in joint family, incompatibility, drinking, smoking or other habits of the husband, financial stresses, psychopathic problems and so on. Why then should dowry be made a scape-goat for every unpleasant situation?

If one goes through the records of matrimonial cases, one would invariably find the plea of dowry harassment either as a charge in divorce cases or a defence in rejoinders to husband's petitions for restitution of conjugal rights. Even when that is not the truth, the parties are advised to incorporate it as a ground as it is the most convenient and potent weapon in the armoury of matrimonial faults.

The worst part of the whole situation is that unscrupulous parties make false complaints under section 304-B and 498-A of the penal code to the police just out of malice, to seek vendetta, or due to wrong advise or instigation. There are several cases in which there have been no problems on account of dowry and also where the girls never wanted to take the matter to the police but were strongly persuaded to do that; and once matters reach police, the whole situation takes an ugly turn. The husband and his parents become culprits in the eyes of the neighbour, the society and the enforcement authorities. A permanent social stigma is attached to the family; the amount of humiliation, tension, harassment and embarrassment is indescribable. The entire family is wrecked. They are socially ostracised; they may be suspended or thrown out of jobs; and in many cases, suffer irreparable damage to mind and body. There have been instances where mother or father have died of shock or committed suicide because the humiliation of a false criminal case was too much to bear. There is no doubt that nothing could be more tragic and shocking than burning or murdering a girl or driving her to suicide by harassing her and the culprits should be deterrently dealt with; but at the same time innocent men also should not be exploited—their number may be small though. If this trend continues it is not unlikely that women themselves might suffer as they would lose credibility and sympathy of the society. Innocent, simple girls are more likely to suffer because of malicious complaints by clever and unscrupulous women.

Role of Parents and Relatives

In this context it may be pointed out that parents and other relations have a very significant role to play in the matter. Rich parents give huge dowries to their daughters and this increases the greed of the other party. They know that the girl's parents can afford it so their demands keep continuing and increasing. This is a vicious circle and at some point of time, problems begin. Besides, if in a family where there are more than one daughters-in-law and the parents of one of them are not rich enough and do not give much, comparisons are made; she is taunted, harassed and tortured. This is true not only in a family but also in a community and society at large. Thus those who give dowry are the one's who perpetrate and perpetuate the evil. Instead of giving dowry in a bid to buy happiness for the girl, they should educate their daughters and make them financially secure.

Parents of the girl sometimes aggravate the situation in another way also—though in good faith and with best of intention. Our social norms being what they are, when a daughter, harassed by her husband and in-laws, comes to her parents for help, advise or shelter, she is given all sorts of sermons like, "Husband is the *parmeshwara* (God) and your place is in his house alone", or "Who will marry your sisters if you come back"? or "What will society say?", and so on. The poor miserable girl meekly walks back. She endures all atrocities till she can and when things become unbearable she puts an end to her suffering by putting an end to her life. If parents give shelter, and consolation to her at a time when she is utterly frustrated many a case of suicide or even murder, would be averted. Are they also not then guilty of abetment?

At times, even in case of minor tensions between the couple, the parents or other relatives of the girl tend to act in haste, or they may be ill-advised to take recourse to police help. There is either acute frustration or anger and they want to "teach a lesson" to the other party or there might even be a genuine feeling that a complaint might set things right and the husband and his family would learn to behave thereafter. The truth however, is the other way round. The moment the matter reaches the police cell or other authorities, the bitterness increases beyond rapprochement. There is always a lurking fear in the minds of the husband and the family of being implicated. It is a vicious circle then—one's action leading to the other's reaction and so on. Leave alone reconciliation, even settlement of other ancillary matters becomes difficult. In the process, all concerned suffer.

Role of Media

The media sometimes plays a very negative role and adds to the already harassed husband by blowing up news of alleged dowry demand or dowry death, out of all proportions. The press sensationalises the news to attract public attention and make it appear as if the man and his family are indeed the criminals. They sit in trial and judgement even before the court process begins. In other words, the verdict precedes trial. The society and women organisations get provoked and the process of rallies, *dharnas* and representations to politicians and judges begins. There are pressures to punish the "guilty" even before guilt is established. This affects the trial as well because, in view of public hue and cry, authorities work under pressure. Also, such media reportings cause irreparable damage to the self-respect and honour of the man and his family. The entire world reads the story where a non-guilty person is projected as the criminal but when after a due trial that person is acquitted and held not guilty, no one would even know. As pointed out by one harassed husband "A" to this author: "The news of alleged 'torture, harassment, and misappropriation of *Istridhan* of wife was published prominently in prominent English and Hindi newspapers of the same group, accusing several members of my family of torturing her. The concerned reporters never bothered to verify the allegations before publishing the 'story'. As the news carried my full name and those of my relatives, designation and the organisation where I was working, it caused irreparable damage to the entire family's image and hard earned reputation in almost every circle we moved. Queries started pouring in following this news. Depressed and disturbed as I was, I immediately registered my protest with the editors of the papers. The newspapers did publish my rejoinder, but after a long time gap and without any apology for publishing an unverified report." As rightly pointed out by this gentleman, one really wonders how many people read the rejoinder and how many of them have a memory sharp enough to re-link and correlate the rejoinder with the original story.

As one husband remarked in a meeting of a men's organisation—the *Patni Atyachar Virodhi Morcha*, 'I loved my wife so much that I had her name tatooed across my arm.... Today I have seven cases pending against me and I know the press will write about me only when I commit suicide'. Another husband said, "under the Dowry Act, with a single stroke, the woman could wreck the lives of all her in-laws. Who will marry my sister when my entire family has been dragged to court by my wife. It does not matter that she has not been able to produce a single witness from around my house to say that she was ill-treated. Judges always believe the woman and even if they don't, society always does."

In a similar hapless pathetic tone, another husband, who reportedly walked in to the meeting with bruises remarked. "My wife hit me ... I don't dare retaliate because she threatens to commit suicide at the drop of a hat. If she does that, I'll spend the rest of my life in guilt and in jail".[12]

The practical enforcement of these beneficial statutory provisions and the working of the various agencies to help women in need has revealed that quite often, the remedy has proved worse than the evil. The idea behind all these measures is to help out women in distress and restore family peace and harmony. Surely it was never the intention of the legislators and administrators that resort should be made to these provisions for even slightest problems which arise because of lack of understanding and adjustment. After all when two stranger families unite into a relationship, a lot of adjustments and compromises are needed. The relationship has to pass through rough storms before it becomes smooth and happy. And if either of them acts in haste or in foolishness, and initiates legal or police action, or even threatens to do that, the relationship is doomed. Families were perhaps less disintegrated and unhappy when such measures of relief were not there. Is it because there was more flexibility in their attitudes; or is it because there were no god-father agencies and laws? Whatever it be, the truth is that resort to these measures without realising the long term consequences is not in the interest of matrimonial stability. What happens is, and this is a deduction from personal experience in handling these cases, that even when problems are peripheral they become aggravated and irreconcilable when help of outside agencies—especially legal and police intervention—is sought. As soon as a woman makes a complaint, the husband and his family are either arrested, may be overnight for two days or even more, or they are interrogated in a very humiliating and insulting manner. This adds fuel to the fire and the already not so happy relationship becomes irreversibly strained. At this juncture all attempts to bring them around are almost futile. The indignity and embarrassment gone through by the man is so grave that he cannot think of rapprochement. Even the parents of the man are not interested to have the daughter-in-law back for fear that she may drag them to the police or criminal courts. Her threats to implicate them in a dowry case, should she decide to do that, is like a Sword of Damocles always hanging over their heads thereby creating disharmony and tension. Thus it becomes almost impossible to mend the relations. Even when parties have not yet fallen apart but there are small bickerings and the wife in the course of a heated argument without really meaning, threatens to end herself or make a complaint, the process of disintegration, fear and tension starts. There is always a lurking fear of her next move. The husband starts thinking on lines of divorce before matters become more complicated for him. In fact these provisions can be used by unscrupulous people to settle personal scores or take vengeance in matters which are entirely unconnected with dowry, etc.

In short, they are great stumbling blocks in reconciliation and have a potential of severe damage to the peace and harmony of marital life if resorted to in a rash, hasty and thoughtless manner.

ENDNOTES

1. AIR 1989 S.C. 1661 at 1669.
2. Section 198-A Criminal Procedure Code, 1973.
3. Inserted by Act No. 43 of 1986.
4. Inserted by Act 43 of 1986.
5. 1987 (1) ALT 762 D.B.
6. *Id.* at 763.
7. *Ibid.*
8. *Id.* at 765.
9. *Id.* at 768.
10. *Id.* at 769.
11. *Id.* at 770.
12. These views were expressed by the husbands at the meeting of the men's organisation.

4

Maintenance and Child Custody

Maintenance

A husband is under a legal, social and moral obligation to maintain his wife. All the personal law statutes as well as chapter IX of the Code of Criminal Procedure[1] provide for it. While maintenance under the personal law can be sought only when there is a litigation under the statute, the Cr. P.C. entitles a wife to claim maintenance even if she is staying separate from her husband without any legal proceedings. Of course she has to prove that there are reasonable grounds for her to stay apart.

The object of maintenance provisions is to prevent destitution and save indigent wives who have no means of sustenance from "seeking sanctuary in the streets". Until a few decades back, a wife was mainly the consort of the husband for the purpose of companionship and propagation. Gradually there has come a change in her status. Laws have been enacted giving her rights in property. She has equal opportunities for education and employment. In fact, during the past few decades, there has been a tremendous change in her social, economic and legal status. Especially in the urban areas, women are fast heading towards financial independence. This is not to convey that she should not be maintained by her husband, but that the law and the courts must adopt an objective approach in the matter. Not always is the husband financially better off than the wife, nor physically or intellectually competent enough to supplement a wife's income by paying maintenance. True, where a wife is uneducated, unemployed and has no financial means to sustain herself, the husband has to and must provide for her whatever is reasonable depending on the facts and circumstances of the case, but if a wife is educated or qualified to take up a job or any work and is physically fit, courts must keep this fact in mind. Likewise, if she is financially independent and there are children, the court should not saddle the husband alone with the liability to maintain children. The duty of maintaining the children should be joint, depending on the income and needs of both the parties. There should be no absolute rule for or against. Maintenance should not be granted as penalty for the husband and a premium for the wife.

There are innumerable cases where a wife who is working and earning claims maintenance from the husband only to harass him and penalise him. There are cases where marriage has lasted for just a few months but the husband has to maintain the wife throughout her life, until she marries again. Likewise, where a husband even proved that the wife has unreasonably deserted him or treated him with cruelty, and he has also got a matrimonial relief on the above grounds, nonetheless courts ordered him to maintain the wife. Is it not cruel on him that he be asked to maintain such a wife so long as he is alive and she remains unmarried, without any fault of his? On the one hand, his married life is ruined by her and over and above that a life-long financial burden is imposed on him to provide for her. Though the law is gradually recognising a woman's parity with man in maintenance claims also but maintenance claims against wives are very rare. Firstly because man still continues to be the primary wage earner in the family. Secondly, even if the wife earns, and earns more than he does, he will consider it as an affront to his dignity to seek maintenance from her, and lastly even if a needy husband does seek an alimony order, the courts and society would view him with sarcasm.

While the law and courts should definitely adequately provide maintenance for wives who are compelled to stay separate or seek divorce from husbands and are unable to earn and maintain themselves, yet, it should not encourage them to become financial drones. Husbands should not be compelled to pay maintenance to a wife who gives up a job so that she can claim maintenance.

It would be pertinent to point out here that the personal law of the Hindus, viz, the Hindu Marriage Act, 1955 and the Parsis, i.e., the Parsi Marriage and Divroce Act 1936 as amended in 1988, provides for maintenance of the husband as well. The Indian Divorce Act 1869 as amended in 2001, the Special Marriage Act, 1954, and the Code of Criminal Procedure do not have any provision for maintance of the husbands, nor does the Muslim Law provide for maintenance for a husband.

There have been some cases during the last few years, very few though, where husbands have sought maintenance under the Hindu Law from their earning wives. In an unreported case in 1986, a district court in Delhi awarded a monthly allowance of Rs. 1,200 to the husband. The parties took a divorce in 1985 after living together for three years. The husband had a house built in Delhi and got it registered in the name of his wife "out of love and affection for her". Some time later, his services were terminated. The house fetched a monthly rental income of Rs. 4,500 which was received by the wife. The husband sought maintenance at the rate of Rs. 2,500 per month. The court found that the husband had no job and no means of supporting himself whereas the wife had sufficient means. Accordingly, a monthly allowance of Rs. 1,200 was awarded in his favour.

In *Lalit Mohan* V. *Tripta Devi*[2] maintenance was granted to the husband who had met with a serious accident as a result of which he lost his mental equilibrium.

In early 1992, newspapers reported a case with headlines "Husband seeks maintenance...", wherein the Supreme Court admitted a special leave petition by a wife challenging a Madras High Court interim order directing her to pay maintenance to her husband. The family court had ordered her to pay Rs. 700 per month to her husband, pending divorce proceedings. The wife's revision petition before the Madras High Court was turned down, hence she filed an appeal before the Supreme Court and got a stay.

According to a very recent report,[3] the Supreme Court has stayed an Andhra Pradesh High Court order directing a working wife to pay alimony to her husband. According to the report, the parties were married in 1984. In 1997 the wife moved out of the house alleging torture. She filed an unsuccessful divorce petition in the family court. The husband sought maintenance and the wife was directed to pay Rs. 3,000 per month as alimony. The High Court upheld this order but the apex court has stayed that order.

Such cases of husbands seeking maintenance from their earning wives is obviously in the increase. One however, still awaits the outcome of the issue in the Supreme Court.

Child Custody

The most traumatic affect of matrimonial dissensions is on children. They are used as a pawn. Under our laws, the father is the natural guardian of a child but in case of separated parents, the custody of the child is given to a parent with whom the welfare of the child lies. The predominant consideration is the welfare of the child and not the superior legal right of either parent. The courts, confronted with custody cases normally give visitation rights and access to the non-custodian parent which is in most of the cases, the father. What happens very often is that the wife tries to create obstacles in the way of access and visitation of the father. Sometimes her fears and apprehensions that the father may kidnap the child or wean him away from her may be genuine, but there are many cases where fathers are emotionally very attached. Denial of access to the child is a source of great anguish and frustration to a father. Our laws as well as the courts are not oblivious of the fact that child needs the love and protection of both the parents for a normal healthy upbringing and in fact court orders are made with that in mind. It is only when such orders are flouted that deep anguish is caused to the husband. While the predominant consideration should always be the welfare of the child, the courts should give due regard to the father's emotions and sentiments as well. The mother should not be allowed to use the child by denying access to the father and thereby inflicting cruelty on him.

ENDNOTES

1. Sections 125 to 128 of the Code.
2. AIR 1990 J & K 7.
3. Reported in *The Hindustan Times* October 1, 2002.

5

Conclusions

Reiterating at the cost of repetition of what has been said earlier, women are undoubtedly the main victims of domestic violence, cruelty and torture and it is to protect their interests that laws have been enacted. What is disturbing however is when such laws are misused and false and malicious criminal cases are filed against a husband and his family to settle scores unrelated to dowry demand or cruelty. This not only causes great harassment to the husband and his family but ruins the marriage and defeats the very purpose behind the protective laws. In fact the misuse of section 498 A of the penal code has become almost proverbial and even the enforcement authorities, viz—the police and the courts, admit that in a very large number of cases, this provision is used as a scapegoat because this is a provision which immediately sets the law and police into action by apprehending the man and other family members named in the complaint by the wife. If this state of affairs continues, a day will come when anticipatory bails will be a part of marriage package. Some safeguards against the unscrupulous use of these provisions need to be provided in order to maintain a balance while guarding the interests of all the parties.

Fine/Damages

The law of civil damages is rapidly expanding with the ever rising complexities of human relationships, and with the social, mental, emotional and physical damage suffered because of certain acts, omissions and behaviours of some. Certain laws and judicial processes, when misused have the potential of harm against whom they are used. Hence, there is a need to provide some damages to the party who has been wronged. In one case, a few years ago, a magistrate in Delhi not only fined and jailed a husband and his parents for demanding dowry but also ordered that out of the fine imposed on them, Rs. 20,000 should be paid to the victim as compensation for the maltreatment and harassment to her by her in-laws.

In *Mukund Martand Chitnis* V. *Madhuri Chitnis*[1] a husband was ordered to pay Rs 30,000 as fine in a conviction under section 498-A, penal code, and rupees one lakh along with unqualified apology in the court to the wife on account of mental stress and agony caused to her by making various defamatory allegations against her.

In *Ranjit Kumar Bhattacharya* V. *Sabita Bhattacharya*[2] the court ordered Rs. 30,000 by way of damages to a "wife" who was induced by a married man to believe that she was his wife. Her claim for maintenance was not allowed as she was not his legal wife but the court felt that the man should not be absolved for his immoral act.

An award of damages of Rs 10,000 was given to a wife against her husband in *Raju* V. *Baburao*[3] because he had filed a petition for divorce against her on false charges of adultery only to assassinate her character. A husband in *Sunil Masih* V. *Elizabeth Daisy Masih*[4] was awarded Rs 50,000 as damages against the wife and her paramour. This was a husband's petition for divorce against his wife, on grounds of adultery under section 10 of the Indian Divorce Act 1869.

In *Augustine* V. *K. Kuriakose*[5] a husband, who along with his parents suppressed the fact that he was impotent was held guilty of fraud and was ordered to pay rupees one lakh to the wife for the fraud which caused great mental agony to the wife.

It is suggested that there should be a provision for awarding damages to a husband and his family if false, frivolous, vexatious and malicious complaints are made against them and they are subjected to humiliation and harassment following such complaints. Though the suffering and trauma in terms of emotional shock, financial loss and disgrace cannot be made up by any amount of money yet, some provision for damages could have a deterrent affect and prevent false complaints and harassment.

In such cases, section 250 of the Cr. P.C. could also be invoked which provides for compensation for instituting complaint or making accusation before a police officer or magistrate against a person without reasonable cause

Punishment

False and malicious complaints made by a wife and her relatives (or for that matter by anybody) must be severely dealt with. If a husband and his family members can be harassed and maligned simply on suspicion pursuant to a complaint, it is desirable that false complainant should be liable to be punished too. In fact a person who knowingly makes a false complaint against another thereby moving the authorities into action, not only causes misery to the accused but wastes the time and resources of the authorities and also makes a mockery of the legal system and the judicial process. Section 211 of the Indian Penal Code provides for punishment of a person who institutes or causes to be instituted false charges against any person with the intention to cause injury. This provision could be used in case of false charges against husbands also.

Insurance against Broken Marriages

Life, physical health and safety, and mental peace have become more vulnerable today than ever before. One of the factors responsible for this is the innumerable laws which have the potential of causing tension, harassment and disturbing peace of mind. In the context of the subject matter in issue, recent developments in law and procedure which are aimed at maintaining family peace and harmony and ensuring protection of the weaker spouse, have proved to be double-edged weapons. Quite often these have not only caused untold harassment to a party against whom they are applied but also boomeranged and gone against the interest of those who are sought to be protected and benefitted by them. In the process the suffering is mental, emotional, financial and physical. We are living in an age when everything under the sun seems to be insurable. Policies covering risk against life, loss of limb, theft, burglary, accident, etc. are well known and so also insurance of crops against vagaries of nature. There have been insurance policies against rain by organisers of outdoor exhibitions against loss due to untimely rain. A test match that was held in India some years back was reportedly insured against bad weather. Agreements to indemnify instrument players for loss due to injury to fingers are known. Pele, the great Brazilian football player, and a few other football players have, it is learnt, insured their legs. Singers are known to insure their voice. A few years back an insurance company in Sweden had announced that it will issue "bad luck insurance policies". If that be so, marriages as well could be thought of being insured as a disastrous marriage is one of the worst species of bad luck entailing physical, emotional, mental and financial suffering. There is hardly a day which goes without print and electronic media reports about dowry harassed wives, torture by in-laws, bride-burning, suicide, and so on. There are also cases, sporadic though but on the increase, where husbands and their family members are being harassed and victimised by false complaints of dowry demands by the wives and their parents. Though no amount of financial cover can restore mental peace and harmony, but it could mitigate the financial burden of the policy holder. Various problems come up in the wake of marriage breakdown like criminal and civil litigation and processes involving heavy expenditures, social stigma, displacement, effect on business and/or job, resulting in heavy financial losses, if it is the husband his liability to provide maintenance to the wife[6] and children, and so on. The fall outs are endless. An insurance cover cannot prevent marital disasters and breakdowns and the emotional trauma that follows but it may to some extent, equip the policy holder to face and fight the situation with comparatively mitigated financial stress. The premium could be fixed depending on factors like education, job, social, cultural and economic background of the parties. Such policies may be obtained before marriage or at the time of marriage. True, there is risk of collusion with parties feigning to have fallen out but then, such risk is inherent in many insurance policies. This could be combated, to some extent at least, by some evidence of broken marriage like correspondence if any, statements of office colleagues, neighbours or friends or relatives, complaints to police station, NGOs or other forums, medical evidence in case of alleged physical assault, litigation, etc.

The idea is perhaps utopian but may be made viable. The time may not be too far.

ENDNOTES

1. AIR 1992 S.C. 1804.
2. AIR 1996 Cal. 301.
3. AIR 1996 Mad. 262.
4. AIR 2001 MP 226.
5. AIR 2001 Mad. 480.
6. The liability to maintain an indigent husband extends to a wife also under several laws, including the Hindu Marriage Act, 1955.

6

Appendices

APPENDIX I

Cases

Case 1

I was married to a daughter of a police sub-inspector in 1984. It was an arranged marriage. Ours was a joint family consisting of my father, mother, widow aunt (father's sister) elder brother and his family. We have a three storied house and were living on ground floor. However, just before my marriage, the top floor was got vacated so that we could live in comfort and privacy. The marriage never had a smooth sailing. On the first night itself my wife complained that we have been given the *barsati* floor to live in which means that the worst share of the property has been given to us. We went to a hill station for our honeymoon but returned within two days because of her non-cooperation and nagging temperament. There used to be quarrels on petty things and she created a nuisance in the family. She became pregnant after three months of marriage and we registered her with one of the best hospitals in Delhi, for check ups and delivery. We tolerated all her tantrums in view of her condition but her behaviour became more and more intolerable. About five months after the marriage one night she took a fruit knife and locked herself inside the bathroom. The whole family was in a panic. The next morning my parents talked to her parents and she went away to her parents house. She never returned for five/six months inspite of my repeated requests. On the contrary she filed a petition for restitution of conjugal rights and also an application for maintenance. I tried to give another chance to the marriage because neither I nor my parents wanted to break the marriage. Things, however, continued the same way. She used to create scenes over trifles. One night there was some altercation over a petty matter and subsequent morning she left the house with some cash and jewellery. Within two days we were called by the police and my father and I were arrested. She filed criminal complaints under section 498-A and 406 of the penal code against us, including my mother. My widowed paternal aunt who was absolutely bed ridden because of severe arthritis since many years, was also implicated. In fact, after she left we had been repeatedly asking the police to collect her *stridhana* from our house and restore it to her and this fact is on record. But my wife and her parents chose to make false complaints and harassed us. As mentioned above, we were arrested under section 498-A and 406. My father, a Government servant, was suspended, though later on his services were restored. He however, suffered a stroke of paralysis because of deep shock. Bad health, coupled with the shock and humiliation amongst his colleagues, subordinates and seniors impelled him to resign from his class I gazetted job. For several years we suffered harassment and embarrassment in courts, apart from heavy expenditure. We continued to put up with everything in the hope that some day there will be an end to our sufferings. However, that was not to be and the unitracked discriminatory and anti-men laws and procedures took their toll. My father got a heart attack and died because of the continuous tension which seemed to have no end. My mother died soon after due to shock of my father's death and my widowed, childless aunt passed away too, within a very short time because she could not bear the loss of his brother and *bhabi* (i.e. my parents) with whom she had spent all her life ever since she became a child widow. After all this also, the attitude of the opposite party continued to be the same for a long time. Ultimately due to the good offices of some well wishers and the intervention of the judge, the matter was settled. I had to pay her Rs. 80,000 to win back my freedom from false and vexatious cases filed against me, apart from the huge amounts I paid by way of fees to the lawyers. Over and above everything, I lost my precious parents. Can any law, or court or money return them to me? Can my lost esteem, emotional trauma and lost years be compensated?

Case 2

I am a doctor belonging to a highly educated and respectable family. I got married to a doctor girl. We were very happy and my parents showered all their love and affection. Being the youngest daughter-in-law, she got the maximum love from everybody. She herself was very attached to them. The most unfortunate tragedy struck the family when seven months after marriage, my wife committed suicide in the hostel room of the hospital she was working in, by injecting some poisonous drug. She was suffering from Endogenous Depression with suicidal ideas. This material fact was completely suppressed from us when the marriage was arranged and even after marriage her parents continued treatment without our knowledge.

Though she was usually tired looking and was introvert by nature, it was only after four months of marriage that she disclosed her mental illness and the treatment she was getting with the help of her parents from a Senior Consultant Psychiatrist at one of the hospitals in Delhi. Before marriage she was treated in that hospitals as out-door patient. All this is on record. When her parents continued treatment after marriage, the doctor advised them that they must get her treatment in the knowledge of her husband, but they still concealed it from me. Only when the doctor advised her electric shock treatment for Endogenous Depression and suicidal ideas, this was brought to my knowledge. I immediately consulted the experts in psychiatry. Thereafter, we were getting her treated at Hospital for Mental Diseases, Shahdara. Besides drug treatment, she was advised psychotherapy sessions on 14 to 15 occasions each of one to two hours' duration. I used to take her for these sessions as and when instructed by the treating doctor. Keeping in view her illness, she was advised by the doctor to stay with her parents who were instructed not to leave her alone and not to handover all medicines to her at a time. On the advice of the doctor, I was taking her to cinema and outings after duty hours to cheer her up and stayed with her at her parents house also on a number of occasions. On the ill-fated day my wife left her parents house, where she was staying for the last 2-1/2 months and was to be on duty at least till evening. However, soon after she left home, her father, mother and brother reached her work-place and searched for her there in the ward and in the hostel. On not finding her there, they reached our house to inquire about her and took me along with them to the hospital. When her friend knocked at hostel room she had already committed suicide. All this strongly suggests that she must have left a suicidal note at her parents house which was suppressed. But to evade their responsibility and accountability, they made out false and malicious allegations of demanding a Maruti car, harassment and abetment of suicide against us.

I was arrested by the police five days after this tragedy though the matter was still pending in the court which had yet to submit its report. I was granted unconditional bail by the High Court after being kept in Tihar Jail for 15 days. To add insult to injury, I was placed under deemed suspension due to this false arrest. The harassment and agony we have all undergone cannot possibly be described in words. This, together with screaming headlines in many national dailies had irreparably damaged our reputation and made us an object of scorn in the eyes of countless people who do not know us personally. This already had disastrous impact on the fair name and good reputation that I had earned among my patients, superiors, colleagues and subordinates alike. The disgrace and denigration coupled with long delays in the trial procedure was too much for my father to stand and in disgust he committed suicide. In his suicide note he has clearly pointed out this as the reason for ending his life.

After all this I have now been clearly acquitted by the court but of what avail? Can my father come back? Can the traumatic period I suffered be made up? Can my lost honour be redeemed? Can my financial losses be compensated? For no fault of mine, we have been wrecked only because of law and court process.

Case 3

I am a doctor. I got married in 1986 to a girl who, it later on transpired, was already married. She however, stated at the time of marriage that she was a spinster.

She was bringing up three children which she said were her sister's but the truth was revealed later. We never pulled on well and she was all the time nagging and suspicious. Her behaviour became intolerable day by day. When I came to know about her earlier marriage, which was still subsisting because she had not obtained a divorce, I lodged a complaint under section 495 of the penal code but no action was taken by police. As a counter, she filed a complaint against me with the dowry cell alleging that I and my mother and sister torture her for dowry. Case was registered against me under section 406 and 498-A IPC. Even though I was ready to return all what I had of hers, I was arrested and put behind bars for 20 days. My case is pending. I have also filed a petition for annulment of marriage.

My life has been wrecked. She has committed a fraud on me by concealing her earlier subsisting marriage and instead has implicated me falsely under section 406 and 498-A. All this has had a very bad affect on my reputation, profession, career, health and self respect.

Case 4

I am a senior Class I officer and a writer on women's issues. I was married in a simple ceremony. Soon after marriage I discovered that my wife got married against her wishes and she told me on the very first night not to try to touch her. I suffered severe torture at her hands during honeymoon where she continued to receive phone calls from the man she had a leaning for. When I objected to this I was severely humiliated. Deeply frustrated and bruised I suffered acute depression and breathlessness and had to be hospitalised at midnight in semi-conscious condition where I was kept on oxygen and glucose for several days. While I was in hospital, she threatened me with dire consequences if I disclosed anything to my parents. Badly shaken, the honeymoon was abandoned and we returned home after I was discharged from hospital. I still made an effort and persuaded her to mend her ways, but in vain. She continued to have affair with her 'friend'. Things became intolerable and I filed a divorce petition. Threats started pouring from her and her relatives to withdraw the petition or in the alternative, to be prepared to face consequences. I informed the police about the threats. As a counterblast, she lodged a report against me and 11 of my relatives including those who were living far away from Delhi, where we lived, under sections 406 and 498-A of the penal code with the crimes against women's cell, and the local police station. She charged us of demanding dowry, misappropriation of her *istridhan* and cruelty. We were called to the police cell several times. We tried our best to convince them that it was not a case of dowry. Even a letter written by the Director of a leading women's organisation who knew me, to the then DCP of the women's cell to look into all aspects of the case in order to get to the truth, yielded no results. Fearing arrest, I and other members named in the FIR got anticipatory bail. She tried to blackmail me and demanded about Rs. 50 lakhs to sign the divorce petition and withdraw the criminal cases. In order to jeopardise my career and malign me in the eyes of my colleagues and officers, she even wrote letters to my office making false accusations against me and my family but she did not succeed in her designs. The case lingered on for over five years. Utterly harassed and frustrated, I finally got rid of her after paying a good, though much below the originally demanded, amount through my nose. A very unfortunate aspect of my case was that the continuous threats from her and her henchmen panicked me to such an extent that I was forced to leave my own house allotted by the office, along with my other family members at midnight. While we remained homeless and spent nights with relatives and friends, the wife enjoyed my official accommodation for full five years till the case was mutually settled.

Case 5

A human is just like any living creature completing its limited span of breaths in a defined time period with a difference that he is bestowed with intellect that could be used in constructive or negative way. Through this intellect the humans have developed a schedule wherein marriage is a subset aimed at channelising the bubbling energies of the youth with procreativity putting locks of responsibility on unreigned horses.

Having established myself in service I was ready for the responsibility of marriage and like any bachelor was blushing my time with my chosen sweetheart. I found my sweetheart was preoccupied with concerns of little consequences for example that she found my mother was not in a good mood, bla bla bla. The intellect was blurred with blind love. These inconsequential concerns were thought by me as childish and immaturish typical of an Indian female. In spite of our meeting sessions which used to be tutorial sessions tutoring my sweetheart about trying to be positive in thinking yet coming events had cast their shadow immediately after marriage when on the very first day she started an argument with my mother in a manner not befitting by any standards to a newly married female who is yet to know the people where she has to live for her life. There was some uneasiness, a sense of fear constantly occupying my mind. This was the beginning of harassment.

The events followed fast. I was looked with suspicion talking to my mother, father or any other relative. Immediately after the marriage, my wife started making complaints about the status of my family. She also started complaining that she felt disgusted and humiliated by marrying me, who is no match to her. Ever since the marriage she started insisting and coercing me to separate from my parents which as per the very norms of the society to which we belong, was regarded as highly unethical and disgraceful. On the very first day when I got an opportunity to meet her alone in a room, she openly declared that she is a modern woman and she hates the traditional life style. She further branded my family as a bunch of orthodox people, who had no manners to live in the modern set up of the society. I was shocked to note that she was not even interested in living in joint family and that I should immediately arrange another independent home for her. She always used to make cutting remarks and used to tell that it was only on the persuasion of her parents that she had agreed to marry. Even during the first month of our marriage, she used to tell me that she knew quite a few ladies associated with women's organisations and any complaint made to them could put the entire family of mine to trouble. She along with her parents always used to extend wild threats to coerce me in order to arrange a separate house and detach myself from my parents.

She had created such an atmosphere in the house that picking up a fight on trivial issues had become a routine for her. On trivial matters, her reactions always used to be hostile and she would start using the abusive and insulting language for one and all in the house. She always used to compare me with one of her college time friend. On many occasions, she openly told that she regretted marrying me on the advise of her parents. She always had most distressful envious and trustless mindset towards me. She had a very strange suspicious nature and she used to fight with me whenever I used to talk to any girl, even during the course of my official duties and had virtually started keeping surveillance on my activities. She even once called her father to our place, who started indirectly threatening us about women cell and were hell bent upon separating me from my parents. My father-in-law took her alongwith on the pretext that she requires some rest and the very next day they called me up at my office again threatening me of women cell.

Looking back it can be clearly said that die was cast by my partner to separate me from my parents which was further supported by her parents, sister of my wife at my in-laws place. The peace inside was shattered. If I had to buy peace for her I had to outweigh my 30-year association with my parents and prove my love. The intellect which I referred earlier had got blurred in my partners mind. The amount of bias was so heavily loaded that she could not even think that in the present times we would need our parents for serving our children, leave aside that we serve them in their old age. The happiness I got from my beloved was that I was restless which I could not share with any body including my mother. I was losing confidence, and weight. The work at private office suffered. I decided to go out for a change, but nothing changed. She used to take some excuses and go to her parent's house. When I used to resent the way she leaves even when I am not present, her sister, parents particularly father insisted indirectly that I live separately. Occasionally on long absences from the house my mother/father used to talk to her parents, they used to threaten them with dire consequences of Women Cell until one day not only me but my brother-in-law and sister who are professionals living a long way were also named as harassers. It was a shock of my life and last nail in the coffin. I decided not to be cowed down by the threats and went for a legal battle which is cast heavily in women's favour. Thereafter the ordeal is still going and I am suffering constantly in terms of money losses, betrayal, and disbelief in human relations.

People say that marriage is a gamble which everybody has to play and participate in. My experience taught me that this is a gamble with difference wherein man is always a loser. I wouldn't like to discourage other guys, but then yes one question remains unanswered as to why it is happening to a very select lot ! So bad and miserable has been my experience about this institution of Hindu marriage that I would like to re-write the Hindu Marriage Act and make it atleast look more respectable so that man also has got something to fall back upon.

May God Bless Everybody....

APPENDIX II

Relevant provisions under the Code of Criminal Procedure 1973 as amended in 2001

Order for Maintenance of Wives, etc.

S. 125: (1) If any person having sufficient means neglects or refuses to maintain:

(a) his wife, unable to maintain herself........

(b) ....

(c) ....

(d) ....

A Magistrate of the first class may, upon proof of such neglect or refusal, order such person to make a monthly allowance for the maintenance of his wife..., at such monthly rate as such Magistrate thinks fit, and to pay the same to such person as the Magistrate may from time to time direct:

Provided.........

Provided further that the Magistrate may, during the pendency of the proceeding regarding monthly allowance for the maintenance under this sub-section, order such person to make a monthly allowance for the interim maintenance of his wife..., and the expenses of such proceeding which the Magistrate considers reasonable and to pay the same to such person as the Magistrate may from time to time direct. Provided also that an application for the monthly allowance for the interim maintenance and expenses of proceeding under the second proviso shall, as far as possible, be disposed of within sixty days from the date of the service of notice of application to such person.

Explanation: For the purposes of this chapter

(a) ....

(b) Wife includes a woman who has been divorced by,

or has obtained a divorce from, her husband and has not remarried.

(2) Any such allowance for the maintenance or interim maintenance and expenses of proceeding shall be payable from the date of the order, or, if so ordered, from the date of the application for maintenance or interim maintenance and expenses of proceeding, as the case may be.

(3) If any person so ordered fails without sufficient cause to comply with the order, any such Magistrate may, for every breach of his order, issue a warrant for levying the amount due in the manner provided for levying fines, and may sentence such person, for the whole or any part of each month's allowance for the maintenance or the interim maintenance and expenses of proceeding, as the case may be, remaining unpaid after the execution of the warrant to imprisonment for a term which may extend to one month or until payment if sooner made:

Provided that no warrant shall be issued for the recovery of any amount due under this section unless application be made to the court to levy such amount within a period of one year from the date on which it became due:

Provided further that if such person offers to maintain his wife on condition of her living with him, and she refuses to live with him, such magistrate may consider any grounds of refusal stated by her, and may make an order under this section notwithstanding such offer, if he is satisfied that there is just ground for so doing.

Explanation: If a husband has contracted marriage with another woman or keeps a mistress, it shall be considered to be just ground for his wife's refusal to live with him.

(4) No wife shall be entitled to receive an allowance for the maintenance or the interim maintenance and expenses of proceeding, as the case may be from her husband under this section if she is living in adultery, or if without any sufficient reason she refuses to live with

her husband; or if they are living separately by mutual consent.

(5) On proof that any wife in whose favour an order has been made under this section is living in adultery, or that without sufficient reason she refuses to live with her husband, or that they are living separately by mutual consent, the magistrate shall cancel the order.

Procedure

S. 126. (1) Proceeding under section 125 may be taken against any person in any district:

(a) Where he is, or

(b) Where he or his wife resides, or

(c) Where he last resided with his wife, or as the case may be with the mother of the illegitimate child.

(2) All evidence in such proceedings shall be taken in the presence of the person against whom order for payment of maintenance is proposed to be made, or, when his personal attendance is dispensed with, in the presence of his pleader, and shall be recorded in the manner prescribed for summons-case:

Provided that if the magistrate is satisfied that the person against whom an order for payment of maintenance is proposed to be made is willfully avoiding service, or willfully neglecting to attend the court, the magistrate may proceed to hear and determine the case ex parte and any order so made may be set aside for good cause shown on an application made within three months from the date thereof subject to such terms including terms as to payment of costs to the opposite party as the magistrate may think just and proper.

(3) The court in dealing with application under section 125 shall have power to make such order as to costs as may be just.

Alteration in Allowance

S. 127 (1) On proof of a change in the circumstances of any person receiving under section 125 a monthly allowance, for the maintenance or interim maintenance or ordered under the same section to pay a monthly allowance for the maintenance or interim maintenance to his wife, child, father or mother, as the case may be, the magistrate may make such alteration... as he thinks fit:

Provided that if he increases the allowance, the monthly rate of five hundred rupees in the whole shall not be exceeded.

(2) Where it appears to the magistrate that in consequence of any decision of a competent Civil Court, any order made under section 125 should be cancelled or varied, he shall cancel the order or, as the case may be, vary the same accordingly.

(3) Where any order has been made under section 125 in favour of a woman who has been divorced by, or has obtained a divorce from her husband, the Magistrate shall, if he is satisfied that:

(a) The woman has, after the date of such divorce, remarried, cancel such order as from the date of her remarriage;

(b) The woman has been divorced by her husband and that she has received, whether before or after the date of the said order, the whole of the sum which, under any customary or personal law applicable to the parties, was payable on such divorce, cancel such order:

(i) In the case where such sum was paid before such order, from the date on which such order was made;

(ii) In any other case, from the date of expiry of the period, if any, for which maintenance has been actually paid by the husband to the woman.

(c) The woman has obtained a divorce from her husband and that she had voluntarily surrendered her rights to maintenance or interim maintenance, as the case may be, after her divorce, cancel the order from the date thereof.

(4) At the time of making any decree for the recovery of any maintenance or dowry by any person, to whom a monthly allowance for the maintenance and interim maintenance or any of them has been ordered to be paid under section 125, the civil court shall take into account the sum which has been paid to, or recovered by, such person as monthly allowance for the maintenance and interim maintenance or any of them, as the case may be in pursuance of the said order.

Enforcement of Order of Maintenance

S 128. A copy of the order of maintenance or interim maintenance and expenses or proceeding, as the case may be shall be given without payment to the person in whose favour it is made, or to his guardian, if any, or to the person to whom the allowance for the maintenance or the allowance for the interim maintenance and expenses of proceeding, as the case may be, is to be paid; and such order may be enforced by any Magistrate in any place where the person against whom it is made may be, on such Magistrate being satisfied as to the identity of the parties and the non-payment of the allowance or as the case may be, expenses due.

Police to Enquire and Report on Suicide etc.

S 174. (1) When the officer-in-charge of a police station or some other police officer specially empowered by the State Government in that behalf receives information that a person has committed suicide, or has been killed by another or by an animal or by machinery or by an accident, or has died under circumstances raising a reasonable suspicion that some other person has committed an offence, he shall immediately give intimation thereof to the nearest Executive Magistrate empowered to hold inquests, and unless otherwise directed by any rule prescribed by the State Governments or by any general or special order of the District or sub-divisional Magistrate, shall proceed to the place where the body of such deceased person is and there, in the presence of two or more, respectable inhabitants of the neighbourhood, shall make an investigation and draw up a report of the apparent cause of death, describing such wounds, fractures, bruises and other marks of injury as may be found on the body, and stating in what manner, or by what weapon or instrument (if any), such marks appear to have been inflicted.

(2) The report shall be signed by such police officer and other persons, or by so many or them as concur therein, and shall be forthwith forwarded to the District Magistrate or the Sub-divisional Magistrate.

(3) When:

i) The case involves suicide by a woman within seven years of her marriage: or

ii) The case relates to the death of a woman within seven years of her marriage in any circumstances raising a reasonable suspicion that some other person committed an offence in relation to such woman: or

iii) The case related to the death of a woman within seven years of her marriage and any relative of the woman has made a request in this behalf: or

iv) There is any doubt regarding the cause of death; or

v) The police officer for any other reason considers it expedient so to do;

He shall subject to such rules as the State Government may prescribe in this behalf, forward the body, with a view to its being examined, to the nearest Civil Surgeon, or other qualified medical man appointed in this behalf by the State Government if the state of the weather and the distance admit of its being so forwarded without risk of such putrefaction on the road as would render such examination useless.

(4) The following Magistrates are empowered to hold inquests, namely any District Magistrate or Sub-divisional Magistrate and any other Executive Magistrate specially empowered in this behalf by the State Government or the District Magistrate.

Prosecution for Offences against Marriage

S 198 A—No court shall take cognizance of an offence punishable under section 498 A of the Indian Penal Code (45 of 1860) except upon a police report of facts which constitute such offence or upon a complaint made by the person aggrieved by the offence or by her father, mother, brother, sister or by her father's or mother's brother or sister or with the leave of the Court, by any other person related to her by blood, marriage or adoption.

Compensation for Accusation without Reasonable Cause

S 250. (1) If, in any case instituted upon complaint or upon information given to a police officer or to a Magistrate, one or more persons is or are accused before a Magistrate of any offence triable by a Magistrate, and the Magistrate by whom the case is heard discharges or acquits all or any of the accused, and is of opinion that there was no reasonable ground for making the accusation against them or any of them, the Magistrate may, by his order of discharge or acquittal, if the person upon whose complaint or information the accusation was made is present, call upon him forthwith to show cause why he should not pay compensation to such accused or to each or any of such accused when there are more than one; or if such person is not present, direct the issue of summons to him to appear and show cause as aforesaid.

(2) The Magistrate shall record and consider any cause which such complainant or informant may show, and if he is satisfied that there was no reasonable ground for making the accusation, may, for reasons to be recorded, make an order that compensation to such amount, not exceeding the amount of fine he is empowered to impose, as he may determine, be paid by such complainant or information to the accused or to each or any of them.

(3) The Magistrate may, by order directing payment of the compensation under sub-section (2), further order that, in default of payment, the person ordered to pay such compensation shall undergo simple imprisonment for a period not exceeding thirty days.

(4) When any person is imprisoned under sub-section (3), the provisions of sections 68 and 69 of the Indian Penal Code (45 of 1860), shall, so far as may be, apply.

(5) No person who has been directed to pay compensation under this section shall, by reason of such order, be exempted from any civil or criminal liability in respect of the complaint made or information given by him:

Provided that any amount paid to an accused person under this section shall be taken into account in awarding compensation to such person in any subsequent civil suit relating to the same matter.

(6) A complainant or informant who has been ordered under sub-section (2) by a Magistrate of the second class to pay compensation exceeding one hundred rupees, may appeal from the order, as if such complainant or informant had been convicted on a trial held by such Magistrate.

(7) When an order for payment of compensation to an accused person is made in a case which is subject to appeal under sub-section (6), the compensation shall not be paid to him before the period allowed for the presentation of the appeal has elapsed, or, if an appeal is presented, before the appeal has been decided; and where such order is made in a case which is not so

subject to appeal the compensation shall not be paid before the expiration of one month from the date of the order.

(8) The provisions of this section apply to summons-cases as well as to warrant-cases.

APPENDIX III

Relevant Provisions under the Indian Penal Code

False Charge of Offence made with Intent to Injure

S 211. Whoever, with intent to cause injury to any person, institutes or causes to be instituted any criminal proceeding against that person, or falsely charges any person with having committed an offence, knowing that there is no just or lawful ground for such proceeding or charge against that person, shall be punished with imprisonment of either description for a term which may extend to two years, or with fine, or with both.

And if such criminal proceeding be instituted on a false charge of an offence punishable with death, imprisonment for life, or imprisonment for seven years or upwards, shall be punishable with imprisonment of either description for a term which may extend to seven years, and shall also be liable to fine.

S 498-A. Husband or relative of husband of a woman subjecting her to cruelty.

Whoever being the husband or the relative of the husband of a woman, subjects such woman to cruelty shall be punished with imprisonment for a term which may extend to three years and shall also be liable to fine.

Explanation: For the purposes of this section, "cruelty" means:

a) any wilful conduct which is of such a nature as is likely to drive the woman to commit suicide or to cause grave injury or danger to life, limb or health (whether mental or physical) of the woman; or

b) harassment of the woman where such harassment is with a view to coercing her or any person related to her to meet any unlawful demand for any property or valuable security or is on account of failure by her or any person related to her to meet such demand.

APPENDIX IV

Author's Proposal for a legislation to protect married men

Protection of Rights and Dignity of Married Men Bill, ... (year)

A Bill to protect the rights and dignity of men during coverture and upon separation and to safeguard their interests.

(1) This Act may be called the Protection of Rights and Dignity of Married Men Act, ...(year)

(2) It extends to the whole of India.

"Married man" means any man who is married according to law and would include:

(i) a man who is living separately from his wife either by a court order or otherwise, and either on his own or on his wife's initiative.

(ii) a man whose marriage has been dissolved by a decree of divorce or annulment.

Protection against Threats

(3) A person whose wife threatens him with suicide or any other act which causes or is likely to cause him insult, indignity, harassment, financial loss and mental and/or physical torture, shall be entitled to seek matrimonial relief in a court of law on that ground.

(4) A wife who attempts to commit suicide shall be liable to be punished under the provisions of the Indian Penal Code for attempt to commit suicide and unless there is cogent evidence to show that the husband's conduct led her to take that step, he shall not be harassed or apprehended by any person, authority, or institution.

Protection against Dowry Allegations

(5) No wife shall, ordinarily, be entitled to bring a charge of dowry against her husband five years after the marriage. Should such a complaint be made, the burden of convincing the court as to why no complaint was made earlier shall lie on the wife.

(6) A wife who makes a false complaint of dowry demand or torture against the husband, shall be liable to be tried and punished under section 211 of the Indian Penal Code (instituting false criminal proceedings against a person) with imprisonment for a term which may extend to two years or with fine, or with both.

(7) A wife who causes the arrest of her husband on charges of dowry, and/or cruelty knowing them to be false, shall be liable to be punished with imprisonment for a term which may extend to five years or with fine or with both.

Such wife shall also be:

(i) estopped from contesting the husband's petition for divorce, and

(ii) debarred from claiming maintenance from the husband.

Maintenance

(8) A husband who is unable to maintain himself may seek maintenance from his wife who is earning.

In determining the quantum of such maintenance, the court shall give due consideration to the needs of the wife and her children.

(9) If a wife seeks maintenance from her husband under the provisions of the personal laws or the Code of Criminal Procedure, the court shall take into account the educational qualifications, health and earning capacity of the wife.

A wife who has been working before and/or after marriage and continued to work until a year preceding the maintenance petition, shall ordinarily not be entitled to claim maintenance from the husband.

Proviso

(i) In construing the term ordinarily, due regard shall be given to a wife's health, family responsibilities and other circumstances which necessitated or prompted her to give up the job.

(ii) A wife on whose complaint the services of a husband have been terminated shall be debarred from claiming any maintenance from the husband.

APPENDIX V

Newspaper Articles

Occupational Hazards of being a Husband*

By Kusum

Apart from the proverbial rolling pin, the wife has other *astras* to hurl at the husband, which includes the threat to drag him and other members of his family to court.

> "Marriage with peace is the world's Paradise; with strife, its life's Purgatory"

Marriages are made to be broken these days. Every marriage has its teething problems but nowadays, the level of perseverance and adaptability of the couple has gone down which has led to the breakdown of family life.

It would not be fair to put the entire blame of a failed marriage on any one party. It cannot be denied that the woman has lived in subservience for long, she has suffered injustice and atrocities. The evil of dowry and the greed of husbands/in-laws have wrecked the lives of many young girls. And this had led to the enactment of special protective provisions for women. However, the working of the legal provisions and court procedures of late are indicative of the misuse of these provisions to harass husbands and the in-laws. Thus provisions which are aimed at safeguarding the interest of woman and maintaining family peace are in a way leading to more distress in families. The number of cases of harassed husbands is definitely on the increase and certain statutory provisions are misused to make the husbands scapegoats. Today, husbandship has become an occupational hazard.

A reference may be made of some of the special penal provisions enacted in the 1980s to safeguard the interests of wives.

---

* The Hindustan Times, January 16, 1997.

Section 498-A of the Indian Penal Code (IPC) says "whoever being the husband or the relative of the husband of a woman subjects such woman to cruelty shall be punished with imprisonment for a term which may extend to three years and shall also be liable to fine."

The explanation to this section defines cruelty as any wilful conduct which drives the woman to commit suicide or causes grave mental or physical injury to her, or harassment of the woman with a view to coerce her for dowry.

The law of evidence, under which as a matter of general rule, a fact has to be provided by the person who makes an allegation, makes as exception in such cases. Thus, if a wife commits suicide within seven years of her marriage, and there is evidence of cruelty, the court may presume, having regarded other circumstances of the case, that the husband or his relatives have abetted the suicide.

Likewise, under Section 304-B of the IPC which provides for punishment for dowry deaths, where the death of a woman is caused by any burns or bodily injury or occurs otherwise than under normal circumstances within seven years of her marriage and it is shown that soon before her death she was subjected to cruelty or harassment by her husband or his relatives for dowry, the presumption is that the husband or his relatives caused the death. The punishment provided for the offence is imprisonment for not less than seven years extendable to life.

Apart from special statutory provisions to protect the incidence of atrocities against women, special police cells have also been set up. The first such cell was set up in 1983 at the police headquarters in Delhi. It was known as the Anti-Dowry Cell. The working of the cell for two years, however, revealed that every problem in the family was attributed to a dowry demand by the husband and his relatives. Every case of suicide or death was considered to be a dowry death. Thus dowry was made a scapegoat. Hence in 1985 the name of the cell was changed to "Crimes against women cell."

Now cases of all kinds of harassment of women can be looked into by this cell. However, in practice, even now, all harassment cases centre around dowry demands. This is the easiest and most potent weapon in the armoury and hence misused in a vast majority of cases. If one goes through the records of matrimonial cases, one would invariably find the plea of dowry harassment either as a charge in divorce cases or as a defence in rejoinders to husband's petitions. The worst part of the whole situation is that unscrupulous parties make false complaints of dowry death or harassment just out of malice, to seek vendetta or due to wrong advice or instigation.

Quite often these beneficial statutory provisions and the agencies set up to help women in distress have made the situation worse. Families were less disintegrated in the absence of these provisions. This is not to blame the law but the manner in which it is being (mis)used with my personal experience in handling matrimonial cases for about two decades. I feel that quite often the problems are peripheral and all that is needed is a tactful handling—giving enough time and opportunity to both the parties to cool off and give vent to their complaints. What happens now is that parties tend to act in haste and approach a cell or some organisation. With all the good intentions of the latter, the matters get aggravated. Rapprochement becomes difficult—almost impossible. At times even when parties have not really fallen out but there are small bickerings and the wife threatens to commit suicide or approach a cell, the husband tries to pre-empt the step and takes all protective steps to guard himself against possible harassment by the wife. The parents of the boy no longer wish to keep their married sons with them because of the lurking fear of being dragged in. In short, the laws and agencies which were set up to safeguard the woman's interest and preserve families are becoming stumbling blocks in reconciliation and have a potential of severe damage to the peace and harmony of marital life if resorted to in a rash, hasty, and thoughtless manner.

*Dowry: The Scapegoat**

By Kusum

Reports on dowry deaths, slogans, rallies and processions against the evil of dowry, seminars and discussions on the subject at different forums have taken the form of an epidemic during recent years. Not only are husbands and in-laws being implicated as murderers or abettors, but even the police personnel are being blamed for indifference, laxity and connivance. True, there may be many instances where innocent brides are being harassed and tortured for dowry but I wonder if any person with perception and sound reason would believe all that is being reported and blown out of all proportions. There may be various circumstances impelling a woman to take the extreme step of pouring kerosene and setting herself ablaze but why make the husband and in-laws the scapegoats? Why cast the burden on them for proving their innocence.

Instances are not lacking where married girls have been driven to commit suicide for reasons of their own and to involve the husband and his parents in such instances would be most unreasonable. The law and the police should undoubtedly take the most stringent view in cases where a woman has in fact been tortured, harassed and maltreated by the husband and in-laws but should not ipso facto view them as the criminals.

More often than not, our social set-up being what it is, the parents of the girls themselves are the persons more responsible for perpetrating this evil and leading to their daughters committing suicide when harassed by the in-laws. When a daughter in difficulty comes to her parents for advice or help the latter, true to their old *dharma*, enjoin upon her to treat the husband as a *parameshwara* and to live in his house and adjust whatever the circumstances. They are afraid of losing their "nose" should a married daughter come back to stay with them. After all, in our

---

* The Hindustan Times, September 14, 1983.

society, loose gossips are more to be heeded than the safety and happiness of a girl after marriage. If parents give shelter and consolation to a girl who is harassed and emotionally in a bad way, many a case of dowry suicide would be averted. In such a state of affairs who are the greater abettors? Let the public be the judge.

Another aspect of this exaggerated reporting and reaction towards death and suicides being imputed to dowry-hungry husbands and in-laws is the difficulty to rapprochement in cases of strained marriage relationships. Almost every marriage has to go through a period of turmoil and tempests before things finally smoothen out, but these days with the charge of dowry being made the scapegoat for every little tension in the family, the man and his family would rather walk out of a marriage than take the risk of restoring a strained relationship and live in a state of lurking fear.

As a reconciliation officer in matrimonial cases pending in various courts, I can speak from personal experience and say that the present attitude towards viewing all bride burning cases as dowry murders or abetment by husbands his parents, is a great stumbling block and deterrent for husbands and in-laws towards accepting the wife back in the marital home lest she should put them in some trouble some day by making a complaint of being harassed or by committing suicide for reasons of her own. In many such cases coming before me the husband and his in-laws have wondered what safeguards the law can provide them with in case of reconciliation is affected and later, due to certain reasons, the wife is not happy and wants to wreak vengeance on them by involving them in a dowry case? I appreciate their apprehension.

It is high time we get over the hangover and view cases of burning, deaths and complaints of harassment by wives in a more logical and objective manner and not label all cases as dowry cases. Imagine the plight of a man and his family who are falsely implicated out of vengeance of some other reason? Taking the law in one's own hand by shouting slogans, breaking window panes of the "culprits" houses, parading them on the streets is ridiculous and offensive. The judiciary has to take a very balanced view and not be weighed and swayed by extraneous matters.

The police can go a long way by apprehending the real culprits but more responsible and expert officers should be put on the task. The subordinate staff is known for its ping-pong attitude. Parents who know that their daughters are being harassed and still do not give them shelter should be equally charged of abetment should their daughters commit suicide.

Last of all, home and institutions should be provided for women in distress. A woman may resort to suicide when she finds that she has nowhere to go and no shelter. Such homes can provide her protection and safety until the tempest dies down and she is in a better position, mentally and emotionally, to steer her way out of the situation.

*Men Too are Victims**

By Kusum

Dowry deaths, rape and eve teasing are subjects which have been blown up beyond all proportions. Death of every married woman is, at the first instance, attributed to a murder by a greedy husband or in-laws or suicide by the girl out of disgust because of torture by them. If the death happens to be by burning, well the odds are 100 percent against the husband and his parents for it is taken for granted that she was deliberately murdered or forced to take the step. The tension, torment and harassment of the husband who is innocent is inexplicable. His image before the society and relations is tarnished once for all and his mind and body emotionally wrecked. Later on he may get out of the soup successfully—may be, but his life becomes miserable with gossips and suspicious eyes all around. His colleagues no longer respect him, his children leave him and the prospects of his remarriage are almost nil.

A cardinal principle of sentencing policy is that it is better to forgive ten suspected criminals than punish one innocent person but in this case, the premise is perhaps the other way round. The moment a death of a house-wife by burning is reported—the husband and his family become culprits in the eyes of the neighbours, society and authorities. Some States probably even have a law, or a proposal, where if the wife dies of burning under suspicious circumstances within a certain period of marriage, the burden of proving that it was not a case of dowry death is on the husband. Protecting the cause of women is a must especially against such heinous acts as putting them or torturing them to death or suicide but is it not equally important to protect the dignity of a man and his family? What is the ratio of innocent husbands is difficult to assess here but it would be unreasonable to label husbands and in-laws as the culprits in all cases. An unscrupulous wife may very well

---

* The Hindustan Times, Septemer 16, 1981.

act obnoxiously and make the husband a scapegoat for some personal vendetta.

As regards rape, its very definition excludes women from within its purview as perpetrators of the crime. Webster's dictionary defines it as an illicit sexual intercourse without consent of the woman, and affected by force, duress, intimidation or deception as to the nature of the act. Similarly, the penal code defines rape as an act with a woman under certain circumstances. No wonder, by the very scheme of nature, a man's physical and biological state, the social norms and environmental set up, he is the one in a position to exploit the woman and not vice versa. That a woman can ever ravish a man was unthinkable some years ago and unbelievable even today. It may, however, be pointed out that there have been incidents where a boy has been ravished by girls. There is an instance which was reported in press some years ago where a group of college girls ravished a shepherd boy to death. Howsoever microscopic such incidents may be but they are no longer improbable.

Eve-teasing is another sphere which no longer remains the exclusive reserve of girls. It is not uncommon these days to come across eves indulging in adam-teasing.

In view of all these developments in our society which are concomitants or outcome of liberation for women, equal opportunities in job and education etc., it is desirable not to take it for granted that in every case reporting rape or torture by dowry-greedy husband or in-laws or death or suicide by burning, the sole culprit is the man. As it is, every incident of burning or death by a married girl immediately finds a prominent place in newspapers in headlines saying "Another dowry death reported". How can the press give a verdict without any investigations having been done in the matter? When found guilty, the offenders should be most severely or rather deterrently dealt with. It is most barbaric to torture a girl or drive her to end her life simply because she does not or is not in a position to meet the demands of greedy people. Nothing could be more barbaric than raping a woman and the culprit deserves to be publicly lynched to death but the chances of innocent men being malafide involved by unconscientious women cannot be ruled out. Ultimately, the court of law acting as a court of justice too, may acquit the man, but who can restore his dignity and respect which has been irreparably impaired by undue publicity and the way the authorities conduct the investigations. Maybe I invite brick-bats from certain sections of the society by writing this piece but justice definitely demands that cases reporting atrocities on women should be investigated with an open mind and not with a presupposition that man is the criminal.

*Anti-dowry Laws Double-edged**

By Kusum

Indian legislation is replete with laws and statutes pertaining to women. There are laws especially made for women and there are general laws with special provisions for women. In order to make the equality clause provided in our Constitution more realistic and meaningful, the Constitution itself permits inequality in as much as it permits the State to make special provisions and laws for women.

After the lapse of a quarter of a century what one finds now is that the balance of the scales has started tilting on the other side. In other words, men are feeling that there is reverse discrimination against them in many ways.

Dowry laws are the most glaring example of the same. Dowry is an evil which should be fought tooth and nail and torturing a woman because of dowry is a sin and crime which deserves the severest punishment. However, our law makers and the organizations who were hell bent on seeing that the dowry provisions were made as stringent as possible are perhaps oblivious of the imperceptible damage that has been done to many women and to the institution of marriage itself.

If legislative provisions alone could eradicate a social evil our society should have been free of the evil by now, but that is not the case. Moreover, powers given to police in this regard are working havoc. The offence should be punishable—severely, deterrently or in whatever way—but surely not the way things have been moving during the past few years.

Writing as one with some experience in handling matrimonial cases it would be no exaggeration to say that the fear of a dowry charge is a major hurdle in the way of reconciling estranged couples. Often the problems with a couple are peripheral and with proper counselling and

* Statesman, November 7, 1985.

reconciliatory efforts the differences can be creased out. But that is being made extremely difficult because of the Damoclean Sword always hanging over the heads of the husband and his people.

There have been scores of cases where out of anger, impulse or rashness the wife, either on her own or on instigation by people around her, rushes to a police station or the anti-dowry cell to make a complaint of dowry demand or torture against her husband or his relations. Police action is quick. They are expected to believe the girl's story and move; the husband and his relations are taken unaware, escorted to the police station and put behind bars.

All pleadings and implorings are in vain until they get out on bail. The matter does not end there. There are lurid reports in the press, termination or suspension of employment. The damage done is irreparable, the agony beyond words. A challan is filed after considerable delay during which period constables hop from one party to the other—for obvious reasons.

The trial of the party begins long before the case goes to court; he is branded a criminal even before the court gives a verdict. Worse, even when no case is proved by the girl and he is acquitted there is no respite. The man's family has been humiliated and their reputation ruined irreparably. Socially they are looked down upon, physically shattered and financially broke.

This is where the girl has already moved the authorities. If after all this, at some stage she realizes the folly of her action, does she stand a chance of reunion with her husband? Absolutely not.

Then there are cases where there is simply disharmony in the relationship. The wife threatens suicide, or announces that she is fed up with everything or in a court petition simply—as a matter of routine—puts a dowry charge among others (because she knows that even if all others fail, this will have the desired result). In such cases also the prospects of bringing about a reconciliation are very remote.

It is unfortunate that quite often even in petitions for restitution of conjugal rights where even a scant reference to dowry is made, the relationship is practically finished from the side of the husband. Where there are other charges or allegations or problems in a marriage, the other party, the husband, is at least prepared to think over them but where dowry is dragged in or there is a likelihood of the same, the doors for rapprochement are sealed for ever, for one is never sure when a dissatisfied wife might use this weapon and put the husband and his parents in soup.

Perhaps writing in this vein, at this point of time when the tide is running high and every unhappy wife is supposed to be a victim of dowry and the protective blanket provision of Section 498-A Indian Penal Code is invoked, might appear eccentric and invite brickbats from various quarters but as an objective assessor of the situation this writer feels that it is time brakes were applied on one-sided sympathy in such cases.

One way to stop false, vexatious and malicious allegations of dowry and the resultant harassment is by making this—i.e. false complaints—as penal as proved torture of a girl by the husband and in-laws on account of dowry (sic). If a man can be sent behind bars even without proof why not the false complainant too? This would have a deterrent and preventive effect on those who are contemplating use of this weapon simply to malign and harass.

The real culprit deserves punishment. Truth is not writ on the face of either party and so nobody's word should be taken for granted. The law, police and society should not proceed on assumptions and act in a way which causes irreparable mental or physical torture to any party.

Beware of Women's Squads*

By Kusum

Women are no longer a husband's doormat. Social awakening, education, economic independence and legislative enactments have revolutionised the women's world. They are equal or even more than equal—to men in almost all respects, barring those in which nature has made them unequal—superior though.

Legislation has been the most potent weapon of social change during the last few decades. Laws giving equal rights and status to women in matrimony, property and jobs were enacted. The Constitution came as a Magna Carta for women conceding much more than equality to them. The Constitution permits special treatment and special laws for the benefit of women even they violate the equality clause under Article 14.

The last few years have witnessed enormous legislative, social and judicial activism in the sphere of protection of women. Dowry has been an evil prevailing in our societies since very long but during the last few years this evil has raised its ugly head beyond all proportions with not a single day passing without headlines in daily newspapers reporting incidence of torture of women and bride burnings due to dowry. This has resulted in stringent anti-dowry laws.

Battered wives and ill-treatment of women were an accepted social more and there was nothing undesirable or horrifying about it but now there are enough and more laws to prevent cruelty to wives. Women were considered not fit and capable to hold properties, they were never independent and were always in tutelage—father, husband and then the son—but now they have equal shares in properties and equal job opportunities too.

However, the practical working of the laws and more particularly the administration of these laws has brought certain very unfortunate facts to limelight. So far as giving

* National Herald, February 2, 1986.

women their due and safeguarding their interest is concerned there can not be two opinions that this was a must and in fact should have come much earlier; but a spirit of over-zealousness has marred the beauty and purpose of these laudable efforts of the legislators and social reformers.

Bride burning and harassment of women because of dowry is the most heinous crime deserving the severest punishment no wonder but the blunder to which we have already reached is—making it a scape goat for all species of unhappiness, and disharmony in the family. The matter does not end here.

As soon as a woman makes a complaint, the husband and his family are doomed. They are arrested, put in jail and dragged in courts. The girl's story is always believed and the other party is roughed up, harassed and tortured like anything. All pleadings and implorings are of no avail. And imagine when after all this torture, disgrace and insult, the other party is acquitted because the charge has not been proved!

Can anything on earth make amends for the shock and disgrace suffered by them? It is not unusual to come across cases where the girl and her parents know well that dowry has never been the cause of unhappiness or domestic quarrels but since that is the most potent weapon which can click in the battle, they resort to it. Their aim is to give a 'Pagra' as is said in Punjab, or a jolt to the boy. This is not to plead that erring husbands and his parents should be leniently dealt with, but that a person should not be 'treated' as an offender unless the guilt is proved in a court of law.

As things stand today, punishment precedes trial, which is intolerable and beyond all ethics. So is the case where other acts of harassment of cruelty are alleged by a woman against the man. It is submitted that police should not be given authority or power to arrest or harass people. Cases should be tried by the courts and the procedure should be very fast.

Also, if guilt is proved, punishment should be severe but to give a long rope to any authority other than courts is not proper. There is every likelihood of manipulation and misuse . A person who is dragged into the net of the police could do everything—even give a birbe—to get out even if he is honest. This way one is compelled to do illegal acts also to save one's skin.

And now, the government has gone still further by introducing special cells to deal exclusively with crimes against women and special flying squads headed by women police. One wonders what is going to be the fate of husbands of unhappy wives or of men in general where a woman wishes to seek vendetta against him!

It is believed that now women welfare bodies have been given a special status in cases of crime against women. Representatives of registered women's welfare groups will be associated with the investigations of every case of dowry harassment, death, rape and other crimes against women. Complaints filed by registered and recognised women's welfare organisations at any police station will be treated as first information reports so that there is no tampering by the police.

It is indeed laudable and praiseworthy that exploited and destitute women should be helped, and perhaps there could be no better forum than women's organisations helping such women but when giving so much authority to any institution one should not ignore the fact that errors in human judgement, human frailties, sentiments and spirit of "teaching a lesson" and vengeance give rise to very unhappy results which are not good for the very cause they are set up for.

To take an instance the object of the anti-dowry laws and their enforcement is to safeguards the interests of women, to prevent torture to them by dowry hungry in-laws and thereby bring peace and happiness in their married life. A question is; has this object been achieved and if so how far? The answer is distressing.

It is common knowledge that every marriage has its teething troubles but ever since the Damoclean Sword of dowry charge has started hanging around every married man, marital adjustments have become difficult. A husband and his parents would rather obtain a divorce and get rid of a nagging wife than live in lurking fear; for even if a woman dies a natural death or commits suicide for some other cause, the chances of their (husband and his people) being dragged in cannot be ruled out if some body is bent upon harassing them.

In cases where parties have already fallen out, chances of reconciliation have become extremely bleak because of such complaints and the consequences that follow and the treatment that is meted out at the hands of the police.

It is suggested that we should go slow with such revolutionary measures and with utmost caution. We should not proceed on an assumption that one party is always right and the other is always wrong. The judgement and the verdict is to be left to the court; the role of the other agencies is only to facilitate investigations and help the court. No party should be roughed up, humiliated or harassed. As things stand today, many innocent people are being tortured because of cunning relations and the undesirable processes which are believed to be the custodians of women's welfare.

If this continues, the day is not far when women will lose sympathy from all quarters, and special protective measures—social and legislative—will be needed to safeguard the interest of exploited and harassed men.

APPENDIX VI

Clippings

Woman inspector arrested for demanding bribe

STATESMAN NEWS SERVICE

NEW DELHI, Sept. 25. — A woman inspector of the Crime against Women Cell of Delhi Police was arrested by the Central Bureau of Investigation for demanding and accepting bribe from a man against whose brother a complaint was pending investigations in connexion with a marital dispute.

A CBI spokesman said the accused, Shoba Chabra, a widow with two children, had demanded Rs 8,000 from the complainant, Naeemuddin, a resident of Farashkhana in the walled city, to help in a case of marital discord against his brother. She was allegedly threatening him with arrest in case the amount was not paid.

The CBI sources added that the bribe amount was later settled at Rs 5,000. The woman inspector was arrested while accepting this amount at her residence in Timarpur yesterday afternoon. The file of the case was also recovered from her residence.

The accused was later released on bail by the CBI on compassionate grounds.

Statesmen, dated 26.9.95

Woman cop held for taking bribe

IE 9·6·96

EXPRESS NEWS SERVICE

NEW DELHI, June 8: The CBI today arrested a lady police inspector of the Women cell for allegedly taking a bribe of Rs 10,000 from a businessman to drop a complaint against him by his wife.

The businessman reportedly had some dispute with his wife who filed a complaint with the cell against her husband in August, 1995.

A CBI spokesman said the lady police inspector Kamla Devi, had since been demanding money from the businessman. The inspector went to the house of the businessman's sister in a South Delhi colony, where the deal was finalised. She was later caught while taking money at Sarojini Nagar market from the businessman.

Indian Express, dated 9.6.1996

□ Helpline

Coming to the aid of the harassed party

SURINDER GOSAIN on the Akhil Bharatiya Patni Atyachar Virodhi Morcha, a unique body, picking up cudgels for harassed husbands

EVERY worm will turn. And harassed husbands too will have their day. Here is a unique organisation which strives to put the man back in his home to rule the roost. The pecking hens may as well scatter, for this body with a three-lakh membership called the Akhil Bharatiya Patni Atyachar Virodhi Morcha cocks a snook at each and every wife, who drags or threatens to drag her husband through courts, police stations and the like.

There were two reasons why R. P. Chug, advocate at the Tis Hazari, set up the harassed husbands club: Suicide notes by three husbands lamenting the absence of any forum to voice their grievance coupled with the increasing incidents of harassment of husbands in the wake of the newly inserted beneficial provisions for women in Section 498 A, Section 406 and 304 B of IPC. These were incentives enough for him to set up a cell to safeguard the interests of men in distress.

Chug began in 1988 on a small note but did not realise that the morcha would get onto a war footing. Today the morcha not only gives legal advice to clients, but lends "organisational support" too. This include dharnas, protests staged from time to time before High Courts, the Supreme Court and even Parliament to highlight the manner and extent of the misuse of the law by wives to harass husbands.

Despite picking up cudgels for men, Chug is clear his morcha stands for making up of marriages, not breaking them. The purpose of the organisation he says is to help husbands and other members of their families too who are maliciously and falsely implicated. Since female members too are dragged to court, the police, women's cells, and the jails (as being part of the husband families) the organisation has a Mahila Front as the women's wing.

The morcha has branches all over the country and in some States the heads of the clubs are police officials. In Delhi alone the membership is 1.5 lakh and include harassed husbands from Class IV employees to professionals, bureaucrats and businessmen.

For an insight into the type of harassments involved here are some case histories available from the morcha's records.

- A victim from Nagpur was called to the police station one fine morning on a false complaint of harassment for dowry by his wife. The victim was humiliated no end when the sub-inspector concerned provoked the wife to spit on her husband's face and slap him with a chappal. This she did proudly. Humiliated, the victim approached the morcha who sought the intervention of the Union Home Minister and the Police Commissioner, Nagpur. The sub-inspector was duly punished.

- Yet another is the pathetic case of a police official's whose son and five female members of the family including his three daughters, one daughter-in-law and wife are in jail because another daughter-in-law succeeded in implicating the family in a dowry case.

- Sometimes, stringent laws backfire. A couple occupying one floor of a house where the in-laws stayed below moved out when problems arose between the wife and in-laws. The in-laws stopped interfering in the couple's affairs after they left, but problems still persisted in the marriage. On the instigation of her mother, the wife filed a case of harassment against her husband and in-laws — just to teach them a lesson. As a result, the entire family including the husband's handicapped sister went to jail. They were released on bail after three days. The wife had not expected matters to get so serious, but things went out of her hand after she filed the complaint.

Hindustan Times, dated 16.1.1997

Unfair advantage

Sir, — If a married woman is harassed by her husband or in-laws, various Government bodies and voluntary organisations come to her rescue. On the other hand, if a man is harassed by his wife or in-laws there is nobody to help him — neither the police nor any voluntary organisation. Interestingly even the law is silent on this issue. Why is there this dissimilarity in laws?

Also while a woman can lodge an FIR against her husband or in-laws as and when she likes men cannot. Why? There should in fact be a time period after separation, say 6 months or 12 minths, during which women can lodge FIR. Today they can do so even after 5-7 years of separation.

If a woman opts for divorce she gets it easily. But if a man does he has to go through untold harassment by Government bodies. he has to return the dowry which is understandable but why does he have to pay the so-called "Istri-Dhan" and cash compensation even if the marriage is annuled within a very short period? The recovery is made on the basis of a list furnished from the woman's side which is always on the higher side and is blindly accepted by Government authorities be it the police or courts. As such women, at large, take undue advantage of these biased laws.

There is an urgent need to amend our laws so that there is no dissimilarity in laws and whosoever (man or woman) is found guilty should be punished. — Yours etc.,

BAKSHI A. K.
New Delhi.

Hindustan Times, Letter to Editor, dated 24.4.1998

Self-immolation bid by 'harassed husbands'

By Our Special Correspondent

GANDHINAGAR, APRIL 27. The Gujarat police on Monday foiled the bid by five people, "suffering from torture by their wives", to immolate themselves and by 10 Dalits to hang themselves in the public in Gandhinagar.

About 150 people, claiming to be members of the 'All India Crime Against Men by Women Sangh', gathered in front of the State Secretariat here. Five of them poured kerosene on themselves and were about to immolate themselves in protest against the Government's "soft corner" for women when the police swooped on them and forced them to disperse.

About 25 persons, including the five who had poured kerosene on themselves, were arrested. Later, a delegation of the 'Sangh' submitted a memorandum to the Chief Minister, Mr. Keshubhai Patel, demanding that the Government scrap some existing laws which provided special protection and privileges to women, which the 'Sangh' believed encouraged women to indulge in husband-bashing. The memorandum also demanded abolition of the women's police cell and the easing of divorce laws to secure "quick remedy" from husband-bashing wives.

Earlier in the day, the police arrested 10 Dalits, from Amreli district in the Saurashtra region, who wanted to hang themselves in public to protest the State Government's failure to restore the lands allegedly snatched away from them by influential land holders. Some 40 families of Dalits from the district were on a dharna in the State capital since March 22. As it failed to move the Government, 10 protesters planned to hang themselves.

The police, however, dismantled the "noose" prepared by the protesters and arrested them.

The Hindu, dated 28.4.1999

A growing number of women are misusing anti-dowry provisions to harass their husbands

By NAMITA BHANDARE

RAMESH LAL, 65, WAS GOING HOME. He had completed the check-in formalities at the Indira Gandhi International Airport in Delhi, stated his meal preferences, got his allotted seat and now looked forward to the flight back to London, where he lives. That's when the police arrested him. "What's this?" asked a stunned Lal. The policeman replied that he had orders to arrest him. "What's my crime?" was the next logical question. "You are charged under Sections 498A and 406." That was a lot of jargon to Lal. The cold reality of the figures sank in slowly when he realised he was being arrested for a crime he had no knowledge of: harassing his daughter-in-law for dowry.

SECTION 498A OF THE INDIAN Penal Code (IPC) was meant to be a weapon of empowerment for women. On the basis of a complaint filed by a woman, a husband and his family members could be packed off to jail. A small step for the abolition of dowry, a giant leap for the women's movement? Hardly. In fact, since the section was introduced in 1984, the number of dowry deaths has trebled: from 52 in 1985 to 151 in 1997. On the other hand, there has been an unforeseen repercussion: use of the law to harass the husband and his family.

Lal's is one such case. Not because he could never have harassed his daughter-in-law, but because she and his younger son had obtained a divorce by mutual consent six months earlier. What's more, the ex-daughter-in-law had signed documents stating that she had received whatever was due to her. The complaint was dismissed once Lal established that his son's ex-wife had concealed her divorce at the time of filing the complaint. But not before he was forced to spend five nights in jail. Why did she do it? "I can't say," says the retired government official. "She probably wanted to humiliate me and extract some sort of revenge for a marriage gone sour."

The law has rebounded in a way never anticipated by legislators. Says K.C. Jain, an advocate who's dealt with over 300 matrimonial cases: "It's supposed to protect women, but nowadays, the law is being used against the husband and his family."

"A woman comes to the Crime Against Women C only if she believes she is being harassed."

YAMIN HAZARIKA, *DCP, Delhi Police*

The provision was made primarily due to the increasing incidence of dowry deaths in the early '80s and the failure of the Dowry Prohibition Act of 1961. But it hasn't helped much. In Delhi alone as many as 16 dowry deaths have been reported till March this year—that's roughly five a month and over one a week. But complaints filed by women under Section 498A in the capital have also gone up: fror in 1985 to 853 in 1997. This yea Crime Against Women Cell of the Police has already received over complaints. Says Yamin Hazarik in charge of the cell: "People are b ning to talk about these things. W are coming out in the open."

Though Hazarika acknowl that a large number of cases regis with her are false, she hastens to ify, "Nobody comes here unless sl lieves she is being harassed." Figu misuse are hard to come by. It do help that the police inquiry i quently superficial and there are gations that the police take adva of their powers to arrest the hus

"The law is supposed to protect women, but it is being used against the husband and his family."

K.C. JAIN, *advocate*

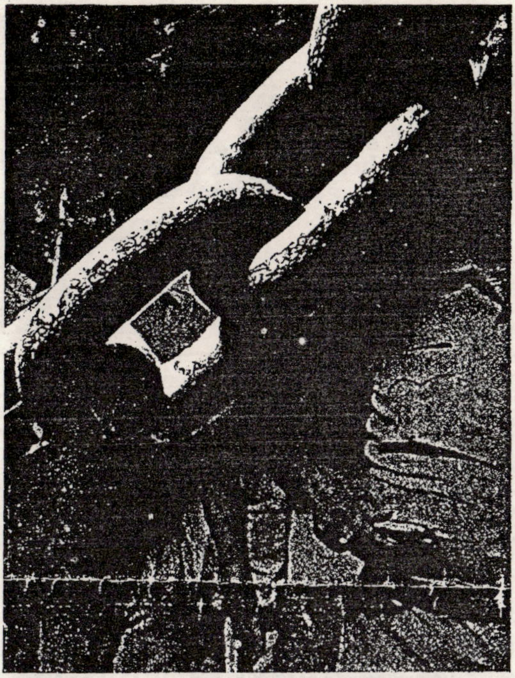

to make a quick buck.

Priya Aggarwal had been married eight months and was pregnant when her husband died. Since she had invested Rs 2.5 lakh in her husband's business, it was decided to settle things once and for all by paying her Rs 3.55 lakh along with 21 gold guineas. Her brother-in-law Vineet Aggarwal, however, says Priya has already taken her jewellery and other possessions, which is denied by Priya. So, when it was time to pay up, Priya changed her mind, filing a case under Section 498A and claiming stridhan *amounting to nearly Rs 25 lakh.*

Women's organisations feel that a woman resorts to 498A only when she finds all avenues of justice closed. "Sometimes," says Padma Seth, adviser to the National Commission for Women, "a woman is left with no other way to make her appeal heard." By law, Priya is entitled to half her husband's estate. It's a claim that could take a couple of decades to settle in the normal course. Whisper "dowry harassment" and things move fast: arrests are made, summons are sent by the police and reputations torn apart. If the complaint is dismissed, the woman is back to square one. She has nothing to lose. Often, lawyers egg on their clients to use this section to get a better settlement: fix errant husbands; send taunting mothers-in-law scurrying for cover; get leverage for the custody of children; demand property rights. "You have to bolster laws relating to women to avoid this," says Geeta Luthra, another advocate.

Nikhil Banerjee knew his wife was having an affair. One day, while his wife presumed he was out of station, Banerjee, loaded with a camera, recorded his wife's escapades. Armed with evidence, he filed a case of adultery and got not only his wife, but the lover arrested too. She responded with a case under 498A. Eventually, the two obtained a divorce by mutual consent.

Advocate Kamini Jaiswal warns that with cases such as these surfacing, the patience of the judges is running out, and it is the genuine victims who will suffer eventually. But then, adultery laws too are discriminatory. Adultery is punishable by imprisonment but only when the husband files a complaint. The wife has no corresponding right—not surprising, since most laws on matrimonial matters were framed in the 19th century and no one has bothered to update them. Maintenance is another matter that has women activists grinding their teeth. Under Section 125 of the CrPC, a Hindu woman is entitled to a maximum of Rs 500 a month. Custody of children often goes to the father. The concept of marital rape is non-existent and often even reports of domestic violence, which come under the general provisions of the IPC, are not taken seriously. Says Nivedita M.V. Monga, project officer with the Multiple Action Research Group: "Even the police tend to say, '*Yeh to ghar ki baat hai* (This is a family matter)'."

Ramesh Gupta, a criminal lawyer, says the law should be changed to recognise that husbands too need protection. "There should be some provision under which he can also make a complaint against his wife." But Monga feels the cases are exaggerated. "Thousands of laws are being misused. Everyone is focusing on this alone because a change in the power structure affects men." It doesn't say much for the judicial system, but for some women misusing the law is their only road to justice.

SECTION 498A OF IPC

- Empowers a woman to get her husband and his relatives arrested for cruel behaviour.
- Offences are non-bailable. Bail can be granted by a magistrate only after the offender has been booked.

DOWRY PROHIBITION ACT

- If a woman dies mysteriously within seven years of marriage, the husband or his relatives can be arrested after investigation.
- Husband and relatives can be jailed for up to three years if they drive a woman to suicide.

Some names have been changed to protect the identity of the persons.

India Today, dated 18.5.1998

NEWS 3

■ Japanese PM impresses kids
■ V-C has given in, say teachers

NEWS

■ Bangl[...] High Con[...] not awar[...] deportat[...]

The Indian EXPRESS
■ NEW DELHI ■ THURSDAY, AUGUST 24, 2000

EX[...]

Domestic violence: Polic[...]

ATIR KHAN
NEW DELHI, AUGUST 23

A DELHI Police report has come down on the proposed Domestic Violence to Women (Prevention) Bill and warned that a provision of the law dealing with this matter is being misused.

The report is prepared by O.S. Sharma, the legal advisor to the Commissioner of Police, and is a feedback to the Law Ministry for the proposed law. An inter-departmental committee comprising of senior police officers — including JCP (Crime) K.K. Paul, JCP (training) Kiran Bedi, Additional Police Commissioner (Crime against Women Cell) D.T. Birde and Additional Commissioner of Police Kanwaljit Deol — has been formed to study the issue in depth.

The report, however, says Section 498-A of Indian Penal Code (IPC) is being regularly misused by married women and their parents in cases of matrimonial discord. Police are already facing a plethora of cases under Section 498-A and the report warns that "there may have been hundreds and thousands of such cases since the enactment of Section 498-A of the IPC."

Sources said the report goes on to

'If a woman says she has been subjected to domestic violence, her husband and members of her family will be in trouble'

term the definition of "domestic violence" in the proposed Bill as "absolutely illegal and against the spirit of (the) family system prevailing in the country since the inception of human kind."

"The proposed Bill, which contains a very vague definition of domestic violence," the report says, "will spoil and ruin the family system in the country in case the Bill is enacted in its existing form."

Criticising the definition of domestic violence in the proposed Bill, the report says: "There is no criteria for domestic violence. If a woman says she has been subjected to domestic vio-

Newsline EXCLUSIVE

lence, (her) husband and family members will be in trouble and thereafter they will not tolerate the woman and the wife."

"The reason for disharmony between the wife and husband," it goes on to adjudicate, "arises only when either the wife is reluctant/refuses to adjust herself in the family circumstances or if the husband feels reluctant to accommodate his wife either on account of

4 | ARTBEAT 5 | SKYWATC

desh
mission
of 300
ons

■ Rev up for Ganesh Chaturthi on September 1 with an exhibition on Gajanan at LTG Gallery

■ FORECAST: Partly cloudy s
showers in some areas.
TEMPERATURE: MAXIMUM 3
normal and MINIMUM 25.3 deg
RAINFALL: Trace. HUMIDITY MAX 92 p.c. and M
SUNSET: 6.51 p.m. THURSDAY SUNRISE: 5.5
MOONRISE: 1.44 a.m. FRIDAY MOONSET: 2.2

PRESSNewsli

e have an attitude, it's in re

unnecessary interference by the parents of the wife or non-cooperative attitude of the wife."

The report says, the Hindu marriage ceremony includes acceptance of seven commitments by the bride as well as the husband. The commitments are

'The proposed Bill which contains a very vague definition of domestic violence will spoil and ruin the family system'

prevailing in society since the institution of marriages.

Defining violence

Under the proposed Bill, domestic violence involves any willful act conduct which:

- Is of such a nature as is likely to drive the woman out of the house or to commit suicide or to injure herself; or
- Cause injury or danger to the life, limb or health (whether mental or physical) of the woman.

It also includes:

- Harassment which causes distress to a woman; or
- Any act which compels the woman to have sexual intercourse against her will either with the husband or any of his relatives or with any other person; or
- Any act which is unbecoming of the dignity of the woman; or
- Any other act of omission or commission which is likely to cause mental torture or mental agony to the woman.

Statistics	1998	1999	2000
498-A cases	771	989	545
Dowry prohibition	10	08	05
Criminal breach of trust	22	20	04
Molestation	653	568	324

(Note: 2000 figures are till mid-August.)

'Impractical, copied from W

■ Domestic violence is not just physical or only because of dow verbal and for reasons other than dowry harassment also. The is first admit that the problem of domestic violence exists. Once th how the problem should be addressed. And go on to think about tem and the infrastructure required to tackle the problem. In cas them beat up their wives. But the problem is still unaddressed. S are more sensitive address the problem. But the issue needs to

■ There are chances that Section 498-A can be misused as it al which could be caused by simple remarks in some cases. And i against the entire family and it is presumed that she is harassed its provision are extremely impractical...According to the old thi say the woman should not approach police for a little tiff in the f according to modern thinking it is not. Unlike others acts such a there is no time limit for the enforcement of this Act.

■ It is easy to enforce laws. But before enacting them their enf ined. We should concentrate on the enforcibility and reduce th we can ensure enforcement and they don't remain on the shel much in it has been copied from the Western world. But it shou are applicable to the Indian environment and attitudes.

Indian Express, dated 24.8.2000

Apex court says false dowry charge is cruelty to husband

By Rakesh Bhatnagar
Times News Network

NEW DELHI: In yet another judgment on "cruelty" as understood in matrimonial cases, the Supreme Court has granted divorce to a man on the ground that he was subjected to "cruelty" due to a false complaint of dowry harassment registered by his wife.

The woman, married for a month, had deserted her husband and lodged a complaint with the police alleging her husband and his parents had been demanding dowry. The husband and her relatives were arrested under section 498 A of the IPC (for causing mental agony over dowry) but they were acquitted both by the trial court and high court as the allegation was proved false.

It was now the husband's turn. He sought divorce on the ground of "cruelty" as he and his family members had undergone mental agony due to the false charges. The wife, in turn, appealed to the apex court.

The husband's lawyer, V Prabhakar, said the marriage irretrievably broke down once his wife chose to cause mental agony to him and his family by filing a false complaint.

In the rare order, a Bench comprising Justice N S Hegde and Justice Dowaiswamy Raju dismissed the wife's appeal. Noting the allegation of cruelty made by the husband, the Bench said: "The trial court, while rejecting other grounds, upheld the complainant's contention that his wife was guilty of the charge of cruelty and granted him divorce."

The Bench added: "Having considered the material, we are of the view that there is no ground to interfere with the concurrent findings of the courts below." In another judgment, the court ruled that an act committed with the intention to cause suffering to the opposite party would be a ground for seeking divorce.

"Cruelty can be said to be an act committed with the intention to cause suffering to the opposite party," the court said.

– Times of India, dated 29.1.2002

Woman gets life term for killing her husband

Press Trust of India
New Delhi, September 12

A LOCAL court on Thursday sentenced to life imprisonment a woman whose husband had given a dying declaration accusing her of setting him on fire with the help of an accomplice. The latter got a life term too.

Additional Sessions Judge D.K. Saini also imposed a fine of Rs 200 each on the two, Shaboo and Gulshan.

They face another month's simple imprisonment if they do not pay the fine.

Their victim, Guddu, had told police that his wife Shaboo poured kerosene on his face after the couple had a fight in May 2000.

"While Shaboo poured kerosene on my face, Gulshan caught hold of me and she threw a lighted matchstick at me," the victim's dying declaration recorded by the police stated.

Guddu died in JPN hospital a few days after his wife set him on fire. A case of murder was registered against Shaboo and Gulshan on the basis of his statement.

The court observed that the testimonies of the defence witnesses could not be trusted because Guddu had been declared fit to give a statement.

Moreover he had identified the assailants in the presence of his uncle and aunt, and there was no reason for the two to depose falsely against the accused, the judge said.

Hindustan Times, dated 13.9.2002

NBT 15-12-02

अवैध संबंधों के कारण खुदकुशी को दहेज हत्या का मामला बना डाला

नगर संवाददाता

तीस हजारी न्यायालय: अवैध संबंधों का पता लगने पर युवती द्वारा की गई आत्महत्या को उसके माता-पिता ने दहेज हत्या का रूप दे दिया। मुकदमे के दौरान अभियुक्तों ने हकीकत अदालत में बयान की। अदालत ने भी अभियुक्तों की बात को विश्वसनीय माना और पति, सास और ससुर को दहेज हत्या के आरोप से बरी कर दिया।

बवाना क्षेत्र के शाहबाद डेरी में 6 अप्रैल, 2001 को ज्योति का शव पंखे से लटका मिला। अगले दिन उसकी माँ, पिता और भाई ने एसडीएम को दिए बयान में ज्योति के ससुराल वालों पर दहेज के लिए विवाहिता की हत्या का आरोप लगाया।

एसडीएम के आदेश पर पुलिस ने दहेज हत्या का मुकदमा दर्ज कर ज्योति के पति राजू, ससुर बैरागी और सास जशोदा को गिरफ्तार कर लिया। मृतका की माँ रमा देवी ने एसडीएम को दिए बयान में कहा कि अभियुक्त दहेज में मोटर साइकिल की मांग कर रहे थे। मांग पूरी न होने पर उसे परेशान किया जाता था। बाद में उसकी हत्या कर दी गई।

अतिरिक्त सत्र न्यायाधीश राकेश कपूर की अदालत में मृतका की माँ, पिता और भाई पुलिस और एसडीएम को दिए बयान पर अडिग रहे। उन्होंने दहेज की मांग दोहराई और कहा कि मोटर साइकिल की मांग पूरी न होने पर ज्योति को मार दिया गया। लेकिन बचाव पक्ष के वकील बी.एस. राना ने जिरह के दौरान मुकदमे का रुख पलट दिया।

उन्होंने कहा कि ज्योति ने दहेज के कारण नहीं, बल्कि अवैध सम्बंधों का पर्दाफाश होने पर आत्महत्या की। उसके अपने जीजा के बड़े भाई रामू से अवैध सम्बंध थे। वारदात के दिन भी वह ज्योति से मिलने आया था।

ज्योति के ससुराल वालों ने दोनों को हाथ में हाथ डाले देख लिया था। कलंकित होने पर उसने अपनी जान दे दी। मृतका के माता-पिता ने भी जिरह के दौरान अदालत में स्वीकार किया कि वारदात के दिन रामू को पुलिस ले गई थी।

पुलिस ने उसे रात को छोड़ दिया। अदालत ने कहा कि नाजायज सम्बंधों का भांडा फूटने पर ही मृतका के माता पिता ने वारदात के अगले दिन दहेज की कहानी गढ़ी।

जबकि वह एक दिन पहले भी अंतिम संस्कार में आए थे। उस समय उन्होंने पुलिस के समक्ष शिकायत दर्ज नहीं की। पुलिस में शिकायत दर्ज कराने में जान बूझकर देरी की गई। अदालत ने यह भी कहा कि मृत्यु से कुछ समय पूर्व दहेज की मांग भी साबित नहीं हो सकी।

Nav Bharat Times, dated 15.12.2002